Wdn

SPECTACULAR
VERNACULAR

LONDON'S 100 MOST EXTRAORDINARY BUILDINGS

DAVID LONG

SUTTON PUBLISHING

First published in the United Kingdom in 2006 by
Sutton Publishing Ltd · Phoenix Mill · Stroud · Gloucestershire

Copyright © David Long, 2006

British Library Cataloguing in Publication Data

A catalogue record for this book is available from the British Library.

ISBN 0-7509-4187-1

In memory of Merton Long

(1926–97)

Typeset in Optima 10.5/13 pt.
Typesetting and origination by
Sutton Publishing Limited.
Printed and bound in England by
J.H. Haynes & Co. Ltd, Sparkford.

CONTENTS

INTRODUCTION

An account of whatever is most remarkable for
grandeur, elegance, curiosity or use.

London and its Environs Described, by R. and J. Dodsley (1761)

The lack of an urban masterplan – although John Evelyn, among others, sought to interest Charles II in one within a few days of the Great Fire – means that in London (in contrast to, say, central Paris, Babylon or even Nazi Berlin) the chief glory lies not in the theatrical effect of triumphant avenues aligned along carefully drafted axes, or meticulously planned grids of street and square, but rather in its many historic and often highly individual buildings.

A few of the strangest and grandest are open to the public, if you know who to ask. But many still remain strictly off-limits, heightening the mystery and sense of secrecy which surround them. Others are buildings people walk by every day, yet these have become so familiar that few stop to consider how curious they are.

Just yards from the Royal Albert Hall, for example, a 300ft tower attracts barely a glance (many locals don't even know it's there). The capital's narrowest building, in Trafalgar Square, is a tiny one-man police station, while its widest – at almost 1,000ft – has been favourably compared to the Winter Palace at St Petersburg.

Others hide behind formal façades, like the tranquil oases of the traditional gentlemen's clubs, for example, whose leafy courtyards and lofty interiors can only be glimpsed through elegant Georgian windows. Or London's great private palaces, those few remaining aristocratic townhouses which still dominate their immediate surroundings.

Still others simply defy any kind of categorisation whatsoever. Transforming the City skyline the Swiss Re Building, or Gherkin, has rapidly become as recognisable as Tower Bridge or the old red Routemaster bus. To the south-west an Arab tent houses the remains of Sir Richard Burton, Victorian explorer and translator of *The Arabian Nights*. And more recently, in Neasden, 2,000 volunteers joined forces to create a vast Hindu temple, which opened in 1995, using thousands of tons of Italian marble, Bulgarian limestone and English oak.

A privately owned tunnel under the Thames (the entrance to which is next to the Tower of London); tube stations nobody's heard of, even though their ticket halls can still be seen at street level; and the incredible complex of more than 6 acres of top secret offices excavated under Whitehall prior to the Second World War – London may be the most visited city on Earth, but it still has the power to surprise.

'**Houses are built to live in, and not to look on; therefore let use be preferred before uniformity'**

Francis Bacon,
Of Building,
1625

1
TUDOR MANOR BORN
An Englishman's Castle

ABBOT'S HOUSE

DEAN'S YARD, SW1

With property prices having long ago replaced the weather as Britain's conversational subject of choice, the debate will presumably never cease about which is the grandest house, the most expensive, the most outrageously opulent, awful or tasteless – and of course who lives in each one. But at least the few who know it can agree on one thing, and that is that hidden away in this secret corner of the Abbey precincts – itself comprising the finest collection of pre-Reformation buildings in the capital – is London's oldest domestic residence.

Today it is the home of the Dean of Westminster, successor to a long line of abbots, but in so far as it is known at all it is probably as the place in which Henry IV went to meet his maker. The first English king actually to have had two English parents, his death came suddenly in 1413. Even then, however, this particular part of the abbey complex was by no means new as it is believed to date mostly from about 1370.

Though luckier perhaps than his French namesake – who having changed his religion three times was eventually stabbed to death by an irritated religious fanatic – Henry IV's reign was nevertheless not well starred from the beginning.

At his coronation he lost a shoe in the procession, from his other foot a spur worked itself loose before falling off, and finally at the banquet which followed a sudden gust of wind succeeded in removing his crown. In such a superstitious place as fourteenth-century England all three were seen as portents of trouble ahead, something only made worse when a fortune teller prophesied that the Plantagenet father of seven would meet his death in Jerusalem.

In the event, of course, Henry was to die without even troubling to set foot in the Holy Land. Instead he was brought into this place, at the time the abbot's lodgings, after being taken ill while at his prayers in the Abbey. Unfortunately, the very place chosen by his attendants (an otherwise appropriately rich, tapestry-hung room used these days for meetings of the Dean and Chapter) was traditionally known as the Jerusalem Chamber. It is said that once this small but suddenly significant fact was revealed to the king he realised immediately he would never leave the place alive.

Sadly, today the lodgings – which include the former abbots' dining hall and the spartan but splendid sixteenth-century Jericho Parlour with its elegant linen-fold panelling – are no longer easy to access. Instead, while meandering through the public parts of the Abbey cloisters, the historic exterior can be glimpsed. The fourteenth-century fabric and some even older stained glass is visible through an ancient stone opening before one emerges into the surprisingly peaceful enclave of Dean's Yard. It is also sometimes possible to see the dining hall, since this now forms part of Westminster School.

ALBANY

PICCADILLY, SW1

Originally the home of the 1st Viscount Melbourne, this intriguing mansion from the 1770s is the work of the great Palladian Sir William Chambers (1723–96) and while the interior has been completely remodelled since that time his chaste façade of mellow brown brick and stone dressings still exudes the perfect aura of a first-rate London residence of the late eighteenth century.

This perception of noble elegance is heightened considerably by the building's unique position, for it stands at the end of its own large but still entirely private courtyard right in the heart of the West End. Opening on to Piccadilly with its buses, motorbikes and non-stop bustle, the yard remains sufficiently tranquil and unspoiled for the sudden arrival at its Tuscan porch of a coach-and-pair to cause no surprise whatsoever.

Albany's current usage is similarly apposite to the period. While other buildings of similar quality in this area have been chopped about, taken over by traditional gentlemen's clubs, or more often simply torn down, Albany – it takes its name from a later owner, Frederick, Duke of York and Albany (1763–1827) – was at the start of the nineteenth century skilfully converted by Henry Holland into smart chambers for bachelors. The perfect base, in other words, for gay young blades. Indeed, even the normally dry Nikolaus Pevsner acknowledges the attractively raffish appeal of the place, describing a 'popular flavour that was slightly disreputable and wholly enviable'.

Little surprise then that more than 200 years after the conversion was completed a set or flat in Albany is still highly sought after. As Macaulay's biographer described it, 'that luxurious cloister, whose inviolable tranquillity affords so agreeable relief from the road and flood of the Piccadilly,' it is hard to conceive of a more perfect central London *pied à terre* than this. It has all the traditional pleasures of clubland with St James's across the street from the front door, and to the rear the expensive amenities of Savile Row, should anyone need to call on his man at Huntsman or Henry Poole.

It is to the rear too that one needs to go to get a real flavour of Albany, namely to its other entrance shown here, which is discreetly tucked away between two tiny but perfect bow-fronted shops at the meeting place of Vigo Street, Savile Row and Burlington Gardens. Providing the perfect short cut through to Piccadilly – at least, 'for those who have the audacity to use it', to quote Charles Dickens – the pristine black-painted entrance gives on to the rope walk, a covered walkway linking the long wings of chambers which Holland constructed on either side of Lord Melbourne's garden. If you have the nerve to try it, however, don't be tempted to run or to whistle since both activities – being still considered utterly ungentlemanly – are even now strictly outlawed within Albany's hallowed precincts.

Despite the absence of a single blue plaque either here or at the front, the list of Albany residents past and present is illustrious. Not just Henry Holland himself, but other leading architects including Basevi and Smirke, and statesmen such as Canning, Palmerston, Gladstone and, more recently, Sir Edward Heath. Also the Lords Snowdon and Clark, Sir Thomas Beecham, numerous writers including Greene, Macauley, Huxley, Priestley, Rattigan and the actress Dame Edith Evans all lived here as did two notable diarists of our own times – Sir Harold Nicolson and the political *enfant terrible* Alan Clark MP. And Lord Byron lived at No. 2a, where he used to box.

CROSBY HALL

CHEYNE WALK, SW3

Described by English Heritage as 'London's most important surviving secular domestic medieval building', Crosby Hall's ongoing journey of more than 500 years from redundant City storehouse to Chelsea's grandest private home must surely rank as one of England's most epic architectural tales. Built between 1466 and 1475 for rich City merchant Sir John Crosby, it was later purchased by Sir Thomas More. It served also as a temporary home for the future Richard III and Sir Walter Ralegh and from 1621 to 1638 was the head office of the Honourable East India Company. Eventually the great hall of this Bishopsgate mansion suffered the very real ignominy of being reduced to a warehouse before it was rescued from the wrecker's ball and moved brick by brick to a new site on the river at Chelsea in 1908.

By chance, what one assumes will be the final resting place for the sole surviving example of a City merchant's domicile was also once Sir Thomas More's garden. That must have doubled Crosby's appeal for its present owner and restorer, Christopher Moran. Having made his fortune in the thoroughly modern world of the insurance markets, Moran makes no secret of his enthusiasm for all things Tudor. Nor of his desire to turn Crosby Hall, with its fine double hammerbeam roof and oriel windows, into the most lavish private address in London.

Certainly Moran has shown great patience, determination and fortitude over what must be one of the most challenging privately funded building projects ever undertaken. For example, when he acquired the freehold in 1989 he had already spent twenty years thinking about the project. Now he is reckoned to have spent seven more years negotiating with the relevant planning authorities, another decade coping with anything up to 100 builders and craftsmen coming in and out each day, and an estimated £25 million on the work itself. That said, other estimates suggest that by the time the eighty-five-room house is finished – and it is not there yet – the final bill will be at least twice as much. Certainly the scale of the project is not hard to grasp when you consider that it takes about ninety minutes to walk round Crosby Hall, a mellow brick and stone assemblage which, like a college quad come to London, now encloses a remarkable Tudor garden.

With its centrepiece a great fountain of the goddess Diana, the gardens were designed by the present Marchioness of Salisbury, her highly detailed work being based on the lessons she gleaned from her own work at Hatfield House. It is clear too that the same painstaking approach has been taken throughout the Hall. Calling on the expertise of dozens of Tudor scholars and scores of specialist builders to conserve and extend this remarkable building, the realisation of Mr Moran's dream has required the relearning of many old skills needed to create a house which is authentically Tudor not just in its overall appearance but also in its execution. Thus the fountain alone took more than three years to create, the solid oak front doors on the river side weigh an incredible 3 tons, and elsewhere people involved in this singular development have had to be taught the lost art of double-struck pointing in order to ensure that the new brickwork looks exactly as it would have done when Sir John Crosby first moved in.

DEBENHAM HOUSE

ADDISON ROAD, W14

Nothing prepares you for this vast peacock-coloured Edwardian extravaganza as it looms above the bustle and hubbub of Holland Park. An extraordinary creation of brilliant blues, greens and creams – and this is only the exterior, you understand – London's most flamboyant Arts and Crafts house was built for the eponymous department store magnate Sir Ernest Debenham by Halsey Ricardo in 1905–7.

Sir Ernest's successful Wigmore Street store was clad in sensible plain white tiles, but here he allowed Ricardo to really let fly with colourful Burmantoft bricks and Doulton tiles, as well as columns, capitals and decorative motifs, all carefully moulded, fired and glazed.

The effect as the house rises out of the trees is both ethereal and whimsical, yet Ricardo's design was essentially a very sound and practical one. One says this because the use of these fashionable ceramics – his 'boldest profession of faith in the use of imperishable glazed materials' – was an attempt to give Sir Ernest's new house a finish which would be impervious to the English weather and proof against the corrosive effects of urban pollution. (Proof also against the enemy as it later stood its ground when in the Blitz a 500lb bomb exploded in the garden.)

Ricardo was a member of the Art Workers' Guild and a sometime partner at Fulham of William de Morgan, and as was common in the Arts and Crafts Movement at this time he recruited numerous friends to work on his hugely elaborate project. Indeed, his accounts book must have read like a *Who's Who* of the Movement, with the intricate plasterwork by Ernest Gimson, the lead rainwater heads made by the Birmingham Guild of Handicrafts, William Aumonier being commissioned to carve much of the main staircase and E.S. Prior to create the coloured glass panels thoughout the house. Similarly, for the entrance hall (and it is said with the help of Debenham's eight children) Gaetano Meo was called on to devise a breathtaking Byzantine setpiece of pierced marble balconies placed beneath a glittering blue and gold mosaic dome.

Finally there was de Morgan himself who was kept busy covering literally every free, flat surface with richly decorated, peacock-blue tiles. Many had been designed especially for a yacht ordered by Tsar Alexander II, the best of them featuring vivid representations of animals, foliage and Tuscan landscapes, also of sailing vessels a good deal more conventional than the Tsar's strange, turbot-shaped *Livadia*. The effect is overpowering – certainly that was Lady Debenham's view – but glorious and uplifting too, not least because the all-encompassing nature of Ricardo's work meant that even the tiniest details were subject to the minutest scrutiny.

Thus, as with Augustus Pugin's decorative work in the Palace of Westminster, everything about Debenham House is bespoke. Everything from the intricate enamel-inlaid brasswork of the Birmingham Guild's ornamental door furniture to the more than two dozen tiled and marbled fireplaces. The domestic technology too, which included an awesome-sounding central cleaning system intended to recover dust from every room using the suction power of a vast engine buried in the basement. Pretty advanced stuff, in other words, though perhaps no more than one might expect from Sir Ernest whose office, being among the first to subscribe to the new Post Office telephone service in 1903, had secured the memorable and historic number 'Mayfair 1'.

FARM HOUSE

FARM STREET, W1

Amid the grand terraces, faceless office developments and Victorian mansion blocks, Mayfair can still throw up the odd residential eccentricity, and arguably none better than this one. Inevitably, it's not quite as old as it looks, and this despite mention in the deeds of a right of way for sheep straight through the middle of the house. In fact it was substantially rebuilt in the early twentieth century by a Mrs Stakosch who favoured a rural Gothic style, complete with half-timbering and heavy panelling.

To her credit she sourced original medieval doors and fixtures to give the place an authentic feel and a century later her attention to detail still shines out. Not just in the impressive oak front door, which is carved on both sides with the heads of the Apostles, but also inside, where Jacobean internal doors close against original linenfold panelling (although the original stone floors have unfortunately been replaced with wide wooden boards).

Its most famous occupant was probably Gloria Swanson – a Carl Jasper mural uncovered in the dining room in the late 1970s shows the Hollywood star in several of her films – but before this it was owned by Gloria Vanderbilt's twin, Lady Furness, who enjoys the distinction of having introduced Wallis Simpson to the Prince of Wales in 1931.

Farm House is surprisingly large too, with a separate staff flat in the basement and above that four reception rooms, a study, a south-facing terrace, six bedrooms and an integral garage. With its many quirky features, such as the oriel window on the stairs (copied from an old London church) and the large first-floor drawing room overlooking the famous Jesuit Farm Street church, it is genuinely charming. As it's also situated in one of Mayfair's quietest streets it's not hard to justify the asking price, said to have been in the region of £4.5 million when it was offered for sale in mid-2005.

FAT HOUSE

GARNER STREET, E2

Architectural jokes generally fail on two scores. The first, and less serious one, is that they are rarely very funny; more serious is the fact that after the pranksters have finished explaining the joke to other insiders, and patting themselves on the back for being so very clever, somebody actually has to move in and live there. The FAT House, though, is quite a good joke, and the architect created it to live in himself, which is more than can be said for the majority of concrete and composite horrors which have been inflicted on the capital in the years since the bombers returned to base.

He is Sean Griffiths, a member of a group going under the rather modish name of Fashion, Architecture & Taste, hence FAT, and while his home dominates the environment at least as much as any 1960s high-rise might do – in this case the environment being an otherwise drab and anonymous street just off the main Hackney Road – it does so in such a way that, even several years after its completion, one still frequently encounters people standing on the opposite pavement with smiles playing on their lips.

Neither does the joke rely simply on his chosen means of construction: Connecticut clapboard colliding with edge-of-town DIY store. In fact what looks like wood is really cement, but the real joke for onlookers has to do with the way the entrance subtly conveys the dual role of the FAT House. In a nod to contemporary urban planning, 2 Garner Street combines both living and working spaces, and the architect has signalled this with an imaginative, double-layered façade. In other words it looks like what it is: a cartoon cottage standing in front of a miniature, multi-windowed office block, the cottage element denoting the designer's family home and the workspace part being a studio for his landscape architect partner Lynn Kinnear.

The FAT House is clever too, much cleverer than one might assume from some of the tricksy little details such as the cloud breaking free from the garden wall, the inverted chimney on the roof of the 'cottage', and the side windows which on closer examination turn out not to be windows at all but rather colourful sequinned panels designed to ripple in the urban breeze.

What Griffiths has produced here is in fact a perfect and extremely practical demonstration of brown-field development, an excellent blueprint for others, the FAT House having been built on the compact site of a former metalworkers' yard. Prior to that the site had been the local dairy – another nice echo of the dual-role theme – and, while given a hardly generous space in which to work, Griffiths has managed to squeeze on to the plot not just a light and spacious home for himself, Lynn and their daughter Lily (with garden or parking), but also the studio with its own entrance for Lynn and her assistants. There is even a separate flat – the rent from which helps to offset the relatively modest building costs.

GIPSY TOWER

GIPSY HILL, SE19

In the absence of an actual castle to call his own, one imagines the average Englishman would settle for a tower. For obvious reasons, though, not many of us get to live out these Rapunzel fantasies, and fewer still within the built-up confines of the London suburbs. Gipsy Tower is one of the rare exceptions, however, the Grade II-listed Victorian Gothic tower being all that now remains of Christ Church on Gipsy Hill near Dulwich.

Designed by John Giles – he had earlier been responsible for the design of the Langham Hotel opposite the BBC in Portland Place – it was completed in 1861 but largely destroyed by arsonists a little more than a century later. After the flames had died down the congregation decided to move into an adjacent building, and for more than a decade this magnificent 120ft tower languished, unloved by any but the bats in its belfry as it gradually fell to pieces.

Looking at it now, a magnificently restored and generously proportioned family home which in 2003 was sold for about £1.2 million, it seems incredible that such a unique property was not snapped up sooner. In fact it took many years before somebody finally stepped up to the challenge, adding to the tower and making of the whole a spacious domicile spread over four floors and an expansive 3,500sq. ft. The careful additions, two plain but angular and well-proportioned towers which huddle in the lee of the original, have some discreet Gothic Revival details of their own, but happily make no attempt to pass themselves off as the genuine article. Instead, and together with a large eight-man lift installed when the conversion was undertaken, they have enabled a romantic but otherwise pretty impractical structure to be remodelled into an elegant and undeniably enviable house.

Complete with a full complement of stone carvings, arches and gargoyles, the accommodation includes a drawing room and library, a music room, a master bedroom with en-suite, three additional bedrooms, a family bathroom and a spacious kitchen and dining area. There is a belfry, of course, which although now minus its bells (and the bats perhaps) has a working clock which still relies on the original 1887 mechanism.

For many would-be tower-dwelling damsels and their rescuers, however, the real selling point must be the view from the castellated roof terrace. Best reached not by the lift but by a traditional winding spiral staircase, and with the base of the tower already at 300ft above sea level, the additional 120ft of the building makes Gipsy Tower one of the highest view-points anywhere within the M25.

HAGAN HOUSE

GOLDEN LANE, EC1

Almost more of a tower within a terrace than just a very narrow house, Joe Hagan's super-slim seven-storey building north of the Barbican in Golden Lane is perhaps the perfect expression of Londoners' general preference for houses rather than flats, regardless of how constrained the resulting living space turns out to be. In fact the house, which has just one room per floor, also finds space for a lift. Not that this formed part of the original, rather minimalist plan when the architect set out to develop the site for himself; instead it was introduced by the new owner when Hagan sold the project on.

Spread over so many floors it is, while narrow, by no means the smallest house in this part of town. (Architects Sarah Cheeseman and Howard Carter of the partnership Thinking Space have squeezed an even smaller one into a similarly tight space on nearby Club Row.) With a footprint barely larger than a normal single-car garage, Hagan's creation nevertheless represents an exercise in the clever utilisation of minimal space which is so impressive as to be almost Japanese.

Hence perhaps the almost Zen-like simplicity of the interiors, which can be readily seen from the street, since the façade of the five principal floors is straightforward floor-to-ceiling glass of a stark simplicity, which in turn serves to further emphasise the challenges of building on such a slender plot. Inside, plain white walls and concealed lighting do much to make the interior spaces feel larger and much airier than in fact they are.

It has to be said too that the challenge of building one of these so-called slot-houses is a huge part of their attraction for the onlooker. Not just because such a project successfully creates out of such unpromising ingredients something more useful and valuable than just a potential fly-tip or another under-utilised parking space. Nor even because when faced with such an example we can all dream about finding another litter-strewn, undervalued pocket of the city and setting out to realise its true potential. Mostly their appeal lies in the ways in which their creators maximise the space, often showing as much ingenuity as those eighteenth-century craftsmen who worked tiny concealed drawers and cubby holes into their escritoires and tallboys, or the creators of the novelty wooden boxes where one must turn this, tweak that, and slide the other in order to gain access.

Thus just as Seth Stein squeezed a car-lift into his Cheval Place mews house, here Hagan was able to incorporate not only a proper roof garden – effectively making another room – but also a miniature front garden in a wide galvanised zinc tub by the front door. Containing climbing plants and bamboos, it serves to slightly soften the lines of all that machined, metal-edged glazing and demonstrates again that, even where space is at such a premium, and property prices so outrageous, utility does not need to be the sole guiding principle.

KENNINGTON PARK COTTAGES

KENNINGTON ROAD, SE11

Now an attractive if slightly scruffy headquarters for the admirable charity Trees For Cities, what is in effect a miniature, vaguely Tudor-style block of flats is a genuine specimen from the 1851 Great Exhibition. All of which makes one rather sad to think how few commuters crawling down the crowded A3 each day even notice it, let alone stop to wonder what it once was.

Originally called The Prince Consort's Model Lodge, it was designed by Henry Roberts. His commission was on behalf of the Society for Improving the Condition of the Labouring Classes, and for its first year it was to be seen close to the Crystal Palace on an adjacent site which had been secured through the offices of Prince Albert in his role as the society's president. In recognition of this an inscription beneath the balcony on the roadside still reads: 'Model houses for families erected by HRH Prince Albert'.

Roberts himself was something of a trailblazer for such reformist housing, and a prime mover for the Society since its founding in the 1840s. In Streatham Street off Tottenham Court Road he was responsible for a much larger model development, built around a central courtyard in 1849, but the Kennington block comprises just four separate dwellings, two on each floor, each containing a parlour or living room, three bedrooms, a lavatory, and a scullery complete with sink and meatsafe, a bin for coal and even a built-in plate rack.

Despite the modest cost of the four units, just £458 14s 7d in total, their construction was advanced for the period and used hollow bricks which the manufacturers claimed were not only cheap but also durable, dry, warm and proof against fire, damp, and even sound. The finish of each brick was sufficiently smooth to render plastering unnecessary and their hollow construction allowed the circulation of warm air from the parlour to heat the airing cupboard.

At the close of the Prince's great exposition, the little building was dismantled and rebuilt by William Higgs on its present site where it was to house a small museum and two members of staff. As an experiment in improving the lot of the urban poor it must be considered a success if only because Roberts' pioneering design was quickly replicated at Cowley Gardens in Stepney and in Fenelon Place in Kensington.

All of which makes its removal to Kennington Park appropriate since, with the exception of the four royal parks, the former common land was for a long time literally the only large open space remaining in the metropolis to which that same urban poor still had free access. It was also the very spot where the Chartists had gathered four years earlier in their bid to build a new radical independent political party dedicated to representing the interests of those very same labouring classes on behalf of whom Roberts had exercised his professional expertise.

LOUDON'S HOUSE

3–5 PORCHESTER TERRACE, W2

Two semis cunningly disguised as a grand and highly distinctive detached villa of 1824, this particular pair is the work of the celebrated landscape gardener John Claudius Loudon, who lived in one half of it with his wife Jane until his death in 1843. A prolific and hugely influential garden writer, his *Encyclopaedia of Plants* (1828) was by far the most comprehensive and biggest selling such publication of its time while *The Gardener's Magazine*, which he founded two years earlier, was the first periodical devoted solely to horticulture.

Loudon was, nevertheless, equally interested in the built environment and was responsible for the introduction of the plane tree into the capital, having recommended it as the ideal species for London's new streets and squares. No less impressively, his 1829 paper 'Hints on Breathing Places for the Metropolis, and for Country Towns and Villages, on fixed Principles' effectively pre-dated the green belt concept by nearly seventy years. Similarly, his ideas for public transport networks, food production and waste recycling in urban areas clearly showed him to be more conscious of what we would call sustainability issues than are many town planners working today.

Something of a restless genius – Loudon was no stranger to bankruptcy – while editing five monthly publications he still found time to invent the system for curving glass which Joseph Paxton employed to create the Crystal Palace and used it himself to produce something similar in the central domed conservatory shown here.

These days the fashion for such constructions is generally held to have been kick-started by Paxton's extensive glass palace of 1851. Prior to this the orangeries of the sixteenth and seventeenth centuries had generally been of brick or stone with large windows and a solid roof, so it had not been possible to build what we might think of as a conservatory until stronger glass became available along with laminated timber and wrought iron. As a result it wasn't until the start of the nineteenth century that the fashion really took hold, when architects such as John Nash, Decimus Burton and Loudon himself started to build such structures on to existing houses.

Interestingly, Loudon's fine house, was restored to its original condition in the early 1970s after it had acquired some clumsy Victorian additions, and the conservatory is now cited as a good example of an extension by City of Westminster planners. But even as they insist that 'the main concerns for the present day property owner in Westminster should be to ensure that a proposed conservatory respects the scale and appearance of the existing property, the street scene and the amenity enjoyed by their neighbours', one strongly suspects that were such an application received now to build such a large, prominent and flamboyant structure, it would be turned down out of hand.

PARK VILLAGE WEST

REGENT'S PARK, NW1

In an age when the terms suburban and speculative builder seem to carry far more negative connotations than positive ones, a trip to John Nash's picturesque model village just beyond the north-eastern boundary of Regent's Park, clearly an influential masterpiece of suburban planning, should help to put things into perspective. Nash (1752–1835) never described himself as an architect, merely a carpenter, and today he is more often thought of as a town planner, although that precise term had yet to be coined in his time. However, he was also a speculative builder, and on an heroic scale, something for which he gained a decidedly murky reputation when it came to his business dealings, although when he died he was considerably in debt.

At Park Village West, though, he definitely deserves a gentler ride, for while Regent Street may be better known, and the great park terraces more often held up as typical examples of his work in London, it was this little development – along with Park Village East on the other bank of the Regent's Canal – which was to prove his most influential. Having planned both developments in 1823, and received the necessary grants from the Crown Estate only the following year, Nash created on two quite unpromising sites a series of self-consciously charming villas – some vaguely vernacular in appearance, others Italianate, still others finished in a loose Gothic style. Far less grandiose and so more intimate than his long terraces, much of their charm today depends on the way in which the individual buildings relate to each other, also to their careful assymetry and, at least at Park Village West, in the gentle, slightly sinuous curve of winding 'village' street.

In this and their obvious artifice, the developments owe less to Nash's other, more formal London plans than they do to his little scheme at Blaise Hamlet near Bristol. Here, a decade or so earlier, he had built a pretty circle of cottages for the retired servants of J.S. Harford, a Quaker banker. These are similarly self-conscious in their pursuit of the quaint and rural and as such no more comprise a real village than do these two in central London.

However, that last point is really irrelevant, for with their creamy stucco and deep eaves these are now genuinely lovely houses in a delightful setting. Unsurprisingly, they quickly set the model for the suburban Victorian villa, and did so for many years to come. Indeed, in their freely applied combination of romantic, Italianate, classical and Tudor details – if not so much in their generous helping of water, trees, ornate gables and balconies – Nash's sophisticated villas created an archetype which in a variety of different guises was to be used by scores of other Victorian housebuilders in both London and the provinces.

It has to be said, though, that this has rarely been achieved with anywhere near the aplomb demonstrated by Nash and his pupil James Pennethorne. While those who came afterwards were merely following fashion, Nash's achievement was to have created working streetscapes which nearly 200 years later are still some of the most engaging and attractive in the whole of London. Externally at least they are also among the most perfectly preserved of the planned architectural enclaves, this despite their particular branch of the canal having now gone – it was filled in, which is a great pity – and at least half of Park Village East having been lost to the railways in 1906.

THE RUSSIAN HOUSE

THE VALE, SW3

After the death of Prince Albert in 1861, one of the more bizarre suggestions mooted by architects was that, rather than being left to languish in Sydenham, his mighty Crystal Palace be up-ended to form a crystal tower more than 1,000ft high. Similarly, well over a century before that, an immense tent erected in St James's Park as part of the celebrations marking the defeat of Napoleon eventually found its way to south-east London where it was reborn as a museum of munitions (q.v.). Meanwhile, in a quiet street just off the King's Road in Chelsea, yet another exotic and supposedly temporary structure has found a more permanent role as a distinctive and now hugely valuable family home.

One of the decidedly more unusual buildings in a borough which could fairly be said to have more than its fair share of eccentric architecture, the little cottage in The Vale is popularly held to be a traditional Cossack *izba* or peasant dwelling. In fact, were this the case, it would have had a roof of rough thatch rather than of tile, probably be whitewashed rather than having its boards painted Suffolk-barn black, and it certainly wouldn't have enjoyed the expensive luxury of the splendid, almost Venetian window this one has, giving those on its first floor a clear view down A.A. Milne's old stamping ground of Mallord Street.

Sitting firmly on its substantial brick plinth, and too useful to be a true folly, this then is definitely a fake. With good reason, though it is a fairly convincing one, having been designed and built by genuine Russians as part of their country's pavilion for an early twentieth-century international exposition. It was later purchased from them, brought in pieces to England and reassembled in the heart of domestic Chelsea; the obvious reward was not hard to foresee and when it went on sale in the late 1990s the *izba*'s combination of location, charm and utter individuality meant it was already worth something in the region of £1.5 million.

Today, but for the *izba*, The Vale is a relatively conventional-looking, well-heeled Chelsea street, but clearly it was never entirely normal, being built over the site of a small deer park – actually it could not have been much more than a small field, given the building which had already taken place in the area. When rising property values started driving out his animals, the owner, a Mr McGuire, apparently sold them on as venison and (as Milton Keynes was to do decades later) replaced his real animals with concrete casts.

ST ALBAN'S TOWER

WOOD STREET, EC2

While declining congregations mean the Church of England has good cause to worry about what to do with the growing number of redundant churches – the majority of which, being architecturally important, are very expensive to maintain – the challenge must in a sense be nowhere greater than it is within the Square Mile. As long ago as the 1970s Church Commissioners were demolishing a church every nine days (ancient buildings in ecclesiastical use were traditionally exempt from the usual planning controls). This being so, with its tiny resident population, an understandable interest in Mammon rather than God, and spiralling land values, the City would have been particularly tempting territory for the hard-pressed Commissioners to cut their costs and release the capital tied up in so many under-used and rapidly appreciating assets.

After all, there are scores of empty churches crammed into its narrow streets and alleys, many of them with strange dedications such as that to St Sepulchre, St Katherine Cree, and St Margaret's Pattens (actually a type of clog). Indeed, Wren alone built more than fifty of them, yet in a post-religious age there is even less need here than in most places for the sorts of arts or community centres which are usually proposed once such buildings slip from their normal use. Not much need for distinctive private houses, either, although this has been the happy fate of at least one of them.

The church in question is St Alban's, which was built on the site of two Roman buildings, possibly second-century barracks, which were discovered in 1962. Wood Street is also said to have been the location of the Anglo-Saxon King Offa's palace and the chapel which he dedicated to the memory of Britain's first martyr, St Alban, in 793.

Rebuilt 850 years later, possibly by Inigo Jones, the church was then destroyed in the Great Fire before being rebuilt again, this time by Wren, who spent £3,165 0s 9d to produce a fair copy of the old church. Extended by Sir George Gilbert Scott in 1858, this final iteration lasted a mere sixty years before being destroyed for the final time, by the Luftwaffe in 1940.

With only the tower left standing, the ruins were eventually cleared away in 1955. With them went the unusual star-shaped vaults and the churchyard, the place where the Worshipful Company of Barber-Surgeons had for years buried the bodies of the many criminals dissected by its members in the name of science.

Today, shorn of all this, the tower looks somewhat forlorn but for its decorated Victorian pinnacles and the small bit of greenery which remains around the base. Standing alone on a small traffic island south of London Wall – with the traffic, the noise, and literally hundreds of office workers able to peer from their workstations in through the delicate tracery of its Gothic windows – it must be one of the least-private private houses, and with the most overlooked roof terrace in all London.

Let us, however, assume that the owner of this unique six-storey, single-bedroom *pied-à-terre* spends most of the daylight hours in an office anyway. And once he or she gets home to the strange seclusion of Wren's tower, the office lights will probably be dimmed, the workers on their way back to the suburbs, and the City returned to peace and quiet. Put like that it sounds rather appealing. Plus, of course, very few of us ever get to live in a genuine Wren.

TROBRIDGE'S CASTLES

BUCK LANE, NW9

After having something of a success with his proto-prefab at the 1920 *Daily Mail* Ideal Home Exhibition, Belfast-born vegetarian Ernest George Trobridge (1884–1942) acquired around 10 acres of gently rolling Middlesex hills. With money he had made designing buildings for the Church of the New Jerusalem, he then set about building his own vision of Olde England on an otherwise uninspiring patch somewhere north of Wembley.

While a follower of the eighteenth-century Swedish mystic Emanuel Swedenborg (1688–1772), Trobridge's preoccupation at this time was with Tudor. Not the real thing, but not the usual between-the-wars stockbroker suburban version of it either. Rather, what he wanted to build was all herringbone brickwork and barleysugar-twist chimneys, and lots of rustic cottages of clapboard and thatch. His approach, however, was anything but old-fashioned, and having patented a new system of compressed greenwood construction using unseasoned elm – plentiful and cheap in those happy pre-beetle times – he set out to produce what he called 'rural cottages in which ancient construction is modified to meet modern needs'.

Unsurprisingly this complete rejection of the architectural mainstream – which at this point was tumbling towards rationalist flat-roof Modern and the aesthetic of the machine age – produced only patronising sneers and sniggers from other architectural professionals. Nevertheless, the power of nostalgia being what it is, the houses themselves proved to be exactly what would-be homeowners wanted and sold extremely well.

Even now, indeed, with the greenbelt gradually being subsumed, it is not hard to understand the almost atavistic appeal of the sort of quasi-rural cosiness promised by Trobridge houses and their bogus antiquity. That said, few then or now would have guessed just how much further back into our architectural past Trobridge was to go when it came to designing some blocks of flats as well. This time he went back another few hundred years, producing a series of slightly bizarre, undeniably camp, battlemented castles complete with arrow slits and even the occasional turret. He even located them close to the summit of Wakeman's Hill, reportedly the highest point in the Borough of Brent, in a bid perhaps to endow them with some measure of authentic castle-like inviolability.

The principal influence for these was said to have been Rochester Castle, but of course the large replacement windows and domestic red-tiled rooflines looming over the top give the game away immediately. Clearly what lies behind is some quite ordinary suburban accommodation, and increasingly even the cement façades are beginning to look more like the sort of thing one finds on a miniature seaside golf course rather than any real attempt at medieval recreation. Far less realistic than his earlier essays in Tudor, in other words, but no less popular for all that and now an important part of Brent's official Buck Lane Conservation Area.

VANBRUGH'S CASTLE

MAZE HILL, SE3

They say nostalgia's not what it used to be and indeed what nostalgia used to be, at least architecturally speaking, was non-existent until Sir John Vanbrugh (1664–1726) – architect, herald, dramatist, soldier and possible spy – conceived a vogue for the medieval in 1717. This he did by building a small castle, on his own account, on a hill in south-east London where the place is still known to many as La Bastille, the name given it by Vanbrugh who had himself been locked up in the famous Parisian stronghold for a period during the early 1690s.

As evidenced by the many roads named after him in the area (Vanbrugh Fields, Hill, Park and Terrace, and even a pub, the Vanbrugh Tavern), Sir John's local associations are strong. For example, he built the castle during his time as Comptroller of Royal Works – he replaced Sir Christopher Wren – when he was director of the adjacent Greenwich Hospital and working nearby at Woolwich for the Royal Ordnance (q.v.).

During this same period he designed several other buildings on neighbouring plots. These included one known as The Nunnery, which was occupied by his younger brother Phillip, a respectable widowed captain in the Navy, and Mince Pie House for another brother, the less respectable Charles. Sadly, though, none of these still stands, the last of them having been demolished as recently as 1911, but the survival of his own little Scottish-style fortress seems assured as it falls within the boundaries of the World Heritage site that is modern Maritime Greenwich.

At the time a friend of Vanbrugh's referred to it as his 'country morsell' – Greenwich was then decidedly rural and in London proper Sir John maintained a town house at Whitehall – and it was noted that the lead roof was designed to be walked upon as even then there was an appreciation of the splendid vistas to be had from Greenwich.

Complete with a defensive ring of walls, bastions and a gatehouse, the castle itself originally comprised just a fairly compact four-square keep, with two circular towers on the southern façade and another one in the centre. It was later extended, though, in a manner more picturesque than symmetrical, this being done in order to accommodate 'two Boys Strong in the Nursery'. Alas, one of his adored children proved to be not quite so strong as he died around his first birthday. Nor indeed was Sir John to enjoy his family idyll for quite as long as he might have wished since he died not long afterwards, of a quinsy (or suppuration of the tonsils) in 1726.

Still privately occupied after his death, Vanbrugh's Castle – the first house ever to consciously seek associations with an earlier, more masculine and more heroic age – was later converted into a school with appropriately military connections, and then finally into flats. It still looks the part, though.

'**All the while the**

Government had

been digging for all

it was worth'

Trench & Hillman,
London Under London,
1993

2
SECRET SUBTERRANEA
Hidden City

EISENHOWER'S WARTIME BUNKER

NORTH CRESCENT, CHENIES STREET, WC1

On some Georgian brickwork in Lord North Street, just off Smith Square in Westminster, one can still discern a painted sign giving directions to a nearby air-raid shelter. It's a nice reminder of grimmer times, an authentic bit of *Dad's Army* if you like, but once you start looking around central London for curious bits of Second World War memorabilia such things pop up everywhere.

By far the most obvious are what remains of HM Government's network of deep-level shelters, not just because the excavations are so vast but also because the above-ground parts are so monolithic, so stark and ugly, and just so plain odd that it's a mystery why more passers-by don't notice them or wonder what they are. Ten were planned and eight built, one underneath Chancery Lane tube station, the rest beneath seven Northern Line stations, each comprising a pair of parallel tunnels an incredible 1,200ft in length with the accommodation spread over two levels. Work on numbers nine and ten was begun but then halted, the first because it was thought to be threatening the fabric of St Paul's and the second, at Kennington Oval, because its proximity to the River Effra made it liable to flood.

Of the eight, four – at Camden, Clapham North and South, and Belsize Park – were intended for civilian use during air-raids and, equipped with latrines, first aid posts and so on, could each accommodate up to 8,000 people. The others, however, were secret citadels for government use: Stockwell providing emergency accommodation for the US military; those at Clapham Common and Chancery Lane set aside for the civil authorities in the event of an attack by V1 or V2 rockets; and the one beneath Goodge Street (opposite) fitted out as General Eisenhower's West End headquarters.

This last one is historically therefore the most interesting; the future US president in his role as Supreme Allied Commander used it as his main command and control centre for all D-Day communications. Indeed, this one even enjoyed the benefit of a direct link to Churchill's famous Cabinet War Rooms, using a Lamson pneumatic tube of the sort one routinely saw employed in department stores until the 1970s.

Plans were drawn up after the war to link them together into a new high-speed tube line, but sadly nothing came of this. Instead Chancery Lane was incorporated into the giant Kingsway telephone exchange, 100ft beneath street level, while the remainder were eventually offered to commercial organisations for use as secure, archival storage. (Interestingly, the lease agreements allow for these to be rapidly reoccupied by the authorities should the need arise; in the meantime the Goodge Street one has been used by Channel 4 to store copies of its programmes.)

Today, spotting where the others are is easy enough, for several of the giant, circular, almost gasometer-like blockhouses which formed the entrances are visible from the A3 as it runs through south London to Clapham. The best is in Chenies Street, however, between Tottenham Court Road and Gower Street, where a pair of linked concrete blockhouses – one like a circular pillbox, the other a slightly taller octagon – tower over a war memorial and completely dominate North Crescent.

Now it is called The Eisenhower Centre, another entrance being in Tottenham Court Road, by the Whitfield Memorial Church. Bizarrely, at some point in the recent past the flat roof of this one was railed in to provide a safe play area for the nearby Fitzrovia Children's Centre. But evidence of its true purpose is still there to be seen in the scratchy remains of a painted sign: —D Property —trance strictly —ohibited —out authority.

GHOST STATION

DOWN STREET, W1

Even discounting the Royal Mail's recently decommissioned 23 miles of private track running dozens of miniature trains from Whitechapel to Paddington, Greater London has around fifty abandoned or 'ghost' stations – which is to say considerably more than many city networks actually have in service. Many can still be seen today. For example, take a look at the entrance to Pizza on the Park next time you're passing Hyde Park Corner and you will notice how it is clad in the same maroon tiles which were traditionally used for the façades of many old underground stations. That's the clue, and once you know what to look for there are several others to find, most famously in this part of town the two at Down Street and Dover Street, both short-lived stops on the Great Northern, Piccadilly & Brompton Railway (now simply the Piccadilly Line), and another close to the Oratory which was known as Brompton Road.

This last was redundant almost as soon as it opened in 1906, and the guard's cry of 'passing Brompton Road' became so familiar that in the 1920s the phrase was even borrowed for the title of a successful West End play. The station itself came back into use in 1939, however, although not as a railway station but rather as a secure operations room for the metropolitan Anti-Aircraft Command. At the close of hostilities it was taken over by the Territorial Army and never returned to its original use.

Dover Street in Mayfair was similarly commandeered, this time to be London Transport's emergency wartime headquarters, although it later found a role as one of London's biggest rubbish chutes when it was used to remove spoil during the excavation of the original Victoria Line.

The most infamous of the ghost stations, though, is probably Down Street, the entrance to which can still be seen round the corner from the Hard Rock Café. It's better known than the others because, while officially it was to become the secure administrative headquarters of the Railways Executive Committee (which was established during the Munich Crisis in order to prepare for a government takeover of the mainline railways in the event of war), it was also the temporary home of Churchill's wartime cabinet. 'A considerable underground office in Piccadilly,' is what Sir Winston called it, 'seventy feet below the surface and covered with high strong buildings.' His home for forty days and nights, it was here that he chaired meetings in its deep bunker until his new, more heavily protected Cabinet War Rooms were ready for occupation.

Apparently Churchill's bath is still down there, near the stairs at one end of the platform, as well as a number of old telephones and other communication equipment which were wired up by the London Midland & Scottish Railway. Similarly, at King William Street in the City – an even older 'ghost' which in 1890 became the northern terminus of the City & South London Railway, the world's first electric tube line – one can still find the tattered remnants of old 'Careless Talk Costs Lives' posters, put up over the platforms during the Blitz when the informal practice of dropping into tube stations while an air raid was on at last became official policy.

LEINSTER GARDENS

BAYSWATER, W2

Several of London's most famous addresses do not really exist. No. 10 Rillington Place became so notorious after John Christie murdered at least eight women there in the 1940s and '50s that it was renamed Custom Close before eventually being demolished. When Conan Doyle installed the world's greatest detective at 221b Baker Street, the actual street numbering only went up to 85. (It wasn't extended until 1930 and today the site is occupied by the Abbey Bank.) Nor will young fans of Harry Potter ever find Sirius Black, or anyone else for that matter, living at 12 Grimmauld Place.

Similarly, no cabbie who knows his way round London is likely to waste his time responding to a request for a pick-up at 23 or 24 Leinster Gardens. That's because, although at first glance these two fine Bayswater terraces look perfectly ordinary, they are in reality just empty façades.

The reason for their existence is something of a strange one. As we have seen, the world's first electric underground railway was the City & South London which linked Stockwell to the City and was eventually incorporated into what became the Northern Line. But more than half a century earlier, City solicitor Charles Pearson had proposed a different form of underground railway, seeking as early as the 1840s to link the mainline rail termini using conventional steam-powered locomotives rather than electric ones.

In running the line from Paddington through Euston, St Pancras and King's Cross to Farringdon, however, the creators of what was to become the Metropolitan Line faced one major problem: what to do with the smoke. Ejecting it into these early, much shallower cut-and-cover tunnels would simply suffocate the crew and their passengers. Nor did Sir John Fowler's design for a new smokeless engine prove workable: using a locomotive powered by red-hot bricks, the so-called 'Fowler's Ghost' made only one brief experimental run before being mothballed. Instead it was decided to route the smoke into large tanks fitted behind each locomotive, tanks which could then be discharged each time one of the new underground steam trains broke cover.

To this end the houses behind these two façades were dismantled in 1867 to make way for the railway when the line was extended from Euston to Paddington. It is now part of the District Line, and trains today can be seen running directly beneath the dummy houses, the space behind still there to provide the perfect spot for those old engines to release the steam and smoke before re-entering the tunnel system.

It's an effective screen as well, since it is only on closer inspection that one notices the absence of letterboxes on the two front doors, the blank, painted-on windows and, from the other side of the street, the absence of any extension into the roof. Perhaps the slightly overgrown trees are a bit of a give-away too, with no residents fretting about their loss of light and calling the council to get them to sort it out.

PUMPING STATION

STEWART STREET, E14

London's decaying docklands were pretty grim in the early 1980s – and not much better once the developers moved in, particularly the London Docklands Development Corporation which was described pretty accurately by one pundit as 'a purveyor of fast junk-architecture to the Isle of Dogs'. Happily things have improved a bit since then, however, the first of the new wave of genuinely worthwhile buildings in the area (as opposed to ones which are merely serviceable) being this stormwater pumping station at Blackwall which was designed by John Outram for Thames Water and the LDDC in 1988.

Just as Sir Joseph Bazalgette had done, trumping function with form at his gloriously flamboyant Byzantine/Moorish Abbey Wood Pumping Station, so this former RAF pilot took a straightforward commission for a working building and used it as a springboard to create a veritable temple to waste. Thus, while the cheerfully playful exterior looks like some crazy, acid-trip doll's house – or something a giant might create with oversized Lego – inside, more than 30ft down, visitors are shown the real reason for the building's existence: to shelter a vast subterranean chamber housing powerful machinery used to pump water into a large surge tank and then out into the Thames.

Clearly classical in its basic proportions, colourfully postmodern in its busy detailing, and unexpectedly bright and eye-catching given its function to perform quietly something which most of us would happily never think about, it has understandably become one of the best-known buildings in Docklands. As a result, tourists on the many boats which in the summer chug from Westminster Pier to Greenwich and back again are among the many who seem always (as the *Sunday Times* once put it) to 'wave and cheer whenever they see an Outram building'.

Even so, and despite its cheery playschool colours, Outram's design is aesthetically very complex, its various motifs borrowed from antiquity and legend and carefully placed on the otherwise plain box of the building to tell a story of river gods and more besides. It is clever in more readily understood ways too – for example in the way the squat proportions express its solidity, durability and utilitarian origins – while many of the apparently ornamental elements are in reality genuinely functional. The two immense columns flanking the entrance, for example, conceal ventilation ducts. Similarly the jet-engine-like roundel suspended from the centre of the pediment houses a fan installed to prevent potentially explosive methane gas from collecting inside this expressive, happy, yet deeply useful, little building.

TOWER SUBWAY

TOWER OF LONDON, EC3

Most Londoners know about the Dartford, Rotherhithe and Blackwall tunnels; a few might even recall the claustrophobic foot tunnel at Greenwich which Sir Alexander Binnie designed to enable south London dockers to walk under the river to work. But not many, one suspects, have heard of Tower Subway which had already closed by the time any of these others were up and running. Built in 1869 by P.W. Barlow, it wasn't the world's first underwater tunnel – the Thames Tunnel at Wapping had opened in 1843 after nearly fifteen years of trials, tribulations and lethal inundations. It is certainly one of the most curious, though, being the only privately owned tunnel under the Thames and, what's more, one which is still in use today.

That said, as it's closed to the public, all one can see of it now is a little circular brick pillar box by the public entrance to the Tower of London which conceals a spiral staircase descending into the gloom. Between it and its twin on the other side of the river in Vine Lane, Barlow's men once tunnelled furiously. Working at a rate of 4½ft a day, they completed the job in an incredible ten months during which time they discovered, among other artefacts, a bag of 300 silver coins from the time of Henry VIII. Sadly for Barlow, though, the bag had to be handed over to the Crown as treasure trove; so too was a considerable amount of his cash in fines and levies as the tunnel entrance was on Crown land.

Once the digging was completed, Barlow started running twelve-seater cable cars or trams through the tunnel, charging a fare of just a penny or tuppence first class. Unfortunately, however, and despite getting his sums right at the outset – using James Greathead's pioneering tunnelling machine the Tower Subway cost only £16,000 compared with the £614,000 Brunel spent at Wapping – his project soon failed. Before long the tunnel was converted into a footway after which more than a million people a year used it, at least until Tower Bridge opened in 1894 and took away the trade.

Thereafter Tower Subway was sold to the London Hydraulic Power Company, which since 1871 used a hidden network of nearly 200 miles of pipes to channel power around London to raise theatre safety curtains, cranes, hotel lifts and so on. Surprisingly LHPC somehow survived until the 1970s – this despite the decidedly Heath-Robinson aspect of its operations, and the eventual triumph of electricity. And once it had gone, a consortium led by the Rothschilds took over the subway (and LHPC's incredibly extensive network stretching from Earls Court to Limehouse), since when the tunnel has been used as a conduit for cable television and other, somewhat more up-to-date, applications.

WATER RING MAIN TOWER

HOLLAND PARK ROUNDABOUT, W14

Almost twice the length of the Channel Tunnel, with its average depth of 130ft actually deeper than most of the London Underground network, and with a diameter large enough to have housed a narrow gauge railway at one time (although this was later taken up so that workers could travel through it by bicycle), the London Water Ring Main now supplies fully half of all London's water needs. Indeed, with a daily capacity of nearly 300 million gallons, it is said it could completely fill the Royal Albert Hall in under three hours.

For such a mammoth construction project – excavated at a cost of more than £250 million and certainly the largest single non-railway tunnelling project ever undertaken in London – it nevertheless remains little known, presumably not just because in Britain we tend to take tap water for granted but also because most of the hard work went on well away from the public gaze.

In fact, apart from the control centre in Hampton, there is really only one place where people get any real idea about what's going on down there, and that's here, at this elegant 60ft stainless steel and glass tower. Sitting on top of one of London's busiest roundabouts, this is the top section of one of a dozen immense vertical shafts which bring water up from the main and into Thames Water's normal below-street distribution network.

At one level the part we can see is just a highly sophisticated piece of engineering, built for a purpose by the Murphy construction group. But at the same time it is also an ultramodern water feature, a kinetic sculpture conceived by two students at the Royal College of Art which has proved sufficiently weird and wacky to hypnotise commuters coming off the West Way with its attractive shifting blue cascades.

It is then something of an exercise in camouflage, Damian O'Sullivan and Tania Doufa's creation concealing a tower which is necessary to accommodate occasional water surges in the main itself. More than this, though, what they have created is a giant barometer, using changes in the water to signal to Britain's weather-obsessed motorists any variation in atmospheric pressure. Hence the use of antifreeze, which by tinting the water blue makes the changing levels more easily visible to passers-by. As a nice green aside, the barometer and the tower's control mechanisms have been designed to be solar-powered, relying on electricity generated on site by using photovoltaic panels fitted to the large solar vane which tops this striking structure.

With good reason, most of the other eleven such shafts are concealed or come up on Thames Water land where limited access means no one is around to notice them. But this one – incidentally the winner of a Royal Institute of British Architects London area regional award in 1995 – serves as a reminder of one of Britain's rare, recent large-scale engineering triumphs. (One shaft, admittedly far less flamboyant, comes up on the Park Lane roundabout for anyone who wants to go and find it.)

WHITEFRIARS CRYPT

MAGPIE ALLEY, EC4

Settling within the Ward of Farringdon Without, London's Carmelite monks – otherwise known as White Friars because they wore a white mantle over their brown habits – had originally arrived in the City of London after being driven out of their Mount Carmel monastery by the Saracens in 1241. Unusually, their priory for a short while retained the right of sanctuary even after the Dissolution. But eventually an order went out to 'pull down to the grounds all the walls of the churches, stepulls, cloysters, fraterys, dorters, chapterhowsys' and by the end of the sixteenth century nothing remained of it – at least above ground.

Indeed, for more than 300 years only a couple of street names (Carmelite and Whitefriars) existed to show the considerable extent of this hitherto sprawling religious complex. But in 1867, following the sale of a very run-down old house in Britton Court, a visitor surveying the property and stumbling down some old stone steps looked at the vaulting of its dingy cellar and proposed that it might in fact be the last surviving remnant of the Carmelites' time in London. Then, in 1927, the tiled paving of a cloister was discovered nearby, under 8ft of spoil beneath the News of the World Building.

In other words, from the time of Henry VIII until that of George V this precious fourteenth-century survivor had been all but forgotten: used as a cellar and then, worse still, a rubbish tip. Today, however, it is remarkably intact. Just 12ft square, it is constructed of worn chalk blocks with a ribbed stone ceiling rising to a shallow dome only a couple of feet or so below ground level, and in one wall a small doorway possibly leads out from the crypt to a concealed exit lying just beyond the monastery wall.

Its survival is fairly miraculous. When the developers moved in and squalid Britton Court was finally swept away the crypt was treated with some dignity, the newspaper's proprietor inserting stone markers into the marble tiling of his reception hall to identify the position of the north aisle of the vanished priory church. Later still, when the press men moved on, the site's new occupiers – international law firm Freshfields Bruckhaus Deringer – went one better, putting the crypt into a specially made steel cradle, raising it up, and rebuilding its foundations before returning the cradle's valuable contents to their 700-year-old home.

So, if you want to see it, just ask. Alternatively, find your way to Pleydell Court behind Fleet Street, turn left into Temple Lane, right down Bouverie Street and left again into Magpie Alley. Named after an eighteenth-century tavern, this is the back of the lawyers' offices at 65 Fleet Street, and if you peer over the railings and into the glass-walled basement you will see the entire, intact medieval structure securely encased within the modern building. There's even a flight of stairs to the left so you can take a closer look.

WHITEHALL UNDERGROUND COMPLEX

STOREY'S GATE, SW1

The existence of a secret tunnel from Buckingham Palace to Heathrow Airport seems highly unlikely, although there is thought to be one running the length of the Mall which was built to facilitate a quick royal getaway to Canada (via Charing Cross Underground, Paddington and Bristol) in the event of a German invasion.

Not that this has ever been confirmed, mind you, although what is clear is that this neck of the woods is honeycombed with tunnels and secret citadels, most of them centred on the vast 6-acre complex of underground government offices which lies beneath Whitehall. Much of it dates back to the 1930s, thereby pre-dating Winston Churchill's time as prime minister. But he must have loved it, being so keen on the idea of waging war from under ground that during the First World War he had even invented his own tunnelling machine as a means of getting troops safely across no man's land.

The Cabinet Secretariat called the network 'the Great Hole in the Ground', and indeed, having begun beneath the Treasury in 1933, it today extends underneath Storey's Gate, Horse Guards Road and Great George Street. What amounts to a giant subterranean office block, it was the work of Army engineer Brigadier James Orr who was appointed OBE for his efforts, although the reason for the award was obviously never given on his citation.

Today its more than 200 rooms are still very much in use, however, and as such are still protected by the great 17ft thick shield of concrete which was constructed in great secrecy by filling in the ground floor of the buildings above. Mostly they are just offices for minor civil servants, but it is conceivable that without Churchill's obvious enthusiasm for all things subterranean we might never have known of their existence. This is because, while no one has stated categorically that it was he who gave the game away, it is certainly true that as the author of the best-selling series, *The Second World War* (specifically in Volume II, in a section headed 'London Can Take It'), he reveals rather more about Whitehall's security arrangements than a mere underling might have got away with at that time.

All of which makes it appropriate that the only part one can easily visit today is the Churchill Museum, which opened in February 2005 in the former Cabinet War Rooms. Fascinating, highly evocative, and with some unique Churchill memorabilia including personal items such as his cigars and a 'siren suit', it is interesting to think that even spread over a generous 10,000sq. ft what one can see here is only a tiny fraction of the whole. Which, in turn, might be only a fraction of what actually exists – since it is plausible that there might one day be more subterranean revelations to come out of Whitehall.

Certainly elsewhere in London there is plenty more. The citadel code-named 'Paddock', which was the Cabinet Office's secret wartime bunker beneath Dollis Hill, is one such. Then there is the 3-mile stretch of tunnel between Leytonstone and Gants Hill which was turned over to Plessey to use as an underground aircraft components factory. And indeed another 'ghost' station, British Museum on the Central Line, which the Brigade of Guards acquired (and still holds) after it closed in 1933.

'**The ceaseless labour of your life is to build the house of death**'

Montaigne,
Essais,
1580

3
MEMENTO MORI
Glory unto Death

BURTON'S TENT

ST MARY MAGDALENE, MORTLAKE

A Roman Catholic churchyard in such an anonymous south London suburb as Mortlake is hardly the place one would expect to find a Bedouin tent. But similarly, once one has read of his adventures in India, Africa and the Middle East, neither is it quite where one would expect to find the mortal remains of an explorer and translator as well travelled, as wild and as exotically cosmopolitan as Captain Sir Richard Burton, KCMG (1821–90).

We have his wife, the former Isabel Arundell, to thank for that, since it was she who ordered that Sir Richard be given extreme unction on his deathbed. Once she had been absolutely forbidden to have the great agnostic and sometime convert to Islam buried in Westminster Abbey, it was also Lady Burton who brought him back here to lie with her.

After his death she fought hard to recreate the man she wished he had been: burning his more obviously scurrilous papers and diaries, a shocking act of vandalism; writing a biography of the good, faithful Catholic husband he had never been; and destroying his collection of pornography, one of Europe's most extensive.

In the end she was true to her husband in one important regard, though, and that was in his wish to be buried with her in an Arab tent. She designed one of marble rather than of canvas, and in fact the iconography is weirdly mixed in that it includes not just a frieze of Muslim stars and crescents but also at the front a depiction of Christ on the Cross. It is in other words a splendidly eccentric structure, and large, too, for such a tiny burial ground, being some 12ft square and 18ft high with the marble cleverly mimicking the drapery of the genuine article. The entrance to the vault itself was long ago sealed shut with cement, but, as is perhaps only fitting for the tomb of someone with Sir Richard's enquiring spirit and showmanship, there is to the rear a large glass window which can be reached by climbing up some iron rungs.

Originally this window was of stained glass and included the Burton family crest. Time or vandalism has done for that, however, but through its plain glass replacement one can still make out the dimly lit interior, with its 'his and her' coffins – one simple, the other more elaborately Victorian and fitted with lanterns – and some interior decoration including a painted crucifix and brass ornamentation. All very strange, rather showy, a bit spooky and decidedly exotic – and one suspects in many ways it's precisely what Captain Sir Richard would have wanted.

RICHARD BURTON

"FAREWELL, DEAR FRIEND, DEAD HERO! THE GREAT LIFE
IS ENDED, THE GREAT PERILS, THE GREAT JOYS;
AND HE TO WHOM ADVENTURES WERE AS TOYS,
WHO SEEMED TO BEAR A CHARM 'GAINST SPEAR OR KNIFE
OR BULLET, NOW LIES SILENT FROM ALL STRIFE
OUT YONDER WHERE THE AUSTRIAN EAGLES POISE
ON ISTRIAN HILLS. BUT ENGLAND, AT THE NOISE
OF THAT DREAD FALL, WEEPS WITH THE HERO'S WIFE.
OH, LAST AND NOBLEST OF THE ERRANT KNIGHTS,
THE ENGLISH SOLDIER AND THE ARAB SHIEK!
OH, SINGER OF THE EAST WHO LOVED SO WELL
THE DEATHLESS WONDER OF THE "ARABIAN NIGHTS,"
WHO TOUCHED CAMOEN'S LUTE AND STILL WOULD SEEK
EVER NEW DEEDS UNTIL THE END! FAREWELL!"

JUSTIN HUNTLY MCCARTHY.

HIGHGATE CEMETERY

SWAIN'S LANE, N6

With stories of stolen bones and sinister exhumations, a tomb shaped like a grand piano, and gruesome rites being performed by the High Priest of the British Occult Society amid the mausolea, Highgate would probably be London's most famous cemetery even without its list of Victorian celebrity residents, ranging from a trio of Rossettis to Radclyffe Hall, and from Karl Marx to Sir Michael Faraday. While, though, Marx's monolithic bust with its rousing battle cry to the proletariat is clearly the most photographed, it is far from being the most interesting of Highgate's many private memorials.

What appears to be the celebrated Coade lion sleeping, for example, is actually 'Nero'. He guards the mortal remains of his owner George Wombwell (1788–1850), menagerist and proprietor of a travelling animal show which at one point numbered John Merrick, the Elephant Man, among its exhibits. Then there is that musical instrument, a monument in stone to concert pianist Harry Thornton, who took time off from his career to entertain the troops in the trenches, only to die in the famous 'flu epidemic of 1918.

The largest and most elaborate, though, is that belonging to *Observer* proprietor Julius Beer (1836–80). J. Oldrid Scott created a giant stepped pyramid topped by a small cross on a spire, the roof a striking blue and gold mosaic, and the interior finished in the *quattrocento* manner; it is modelled on the tomb of King Mausolus at Halicarnassus in Turkey – one the Seven Wonders of the Ancient World.

Even this monster, however, is dwarfed by the public mausoleums which surround it. The cemetery having been built on the site of a mansion belonging to Sir William Ashhurst (Lord Mayor of London in 1693), the Circle of Lebanon was built around a vast cedar growing in the grounds. It accommodates the dead in a series of catacombs built either side of a circular passageway, dozens of coffins being stacked up on stone shelves behind iron doors. It is best reached via Egyptian Avenue, this 'Gateway to the City of the Dead' being approached through an arch flanked by Egyptian obelisks and lotus-decorated columns. Finally, looking out over the circle, is the even grander Terrace Catacombs where – as Beer set out to prove – the well-heeled could build as big, as bold and as brash as they were able to afford.

With its exotic architecture, picturesque layout of terraces and circular walks – and as so many of the famous names among the 166,000 dead bear witness – this atmospheric quarter either side of Swain's Lane was an immediate success when it first opened for business in 1839. It was so successful that *The Lady* reported 'the aspect of death is softened in such a place', while another newspaper confidently predicted it would 'excite some envy among its competitors'. But fashions move on, even in death, and as fewer bodies arrived so the money to maintain it began to run out. Eventually Highgate's glories began to crumble, gradually disappearing beneath the ivy and the undergrowth, the monuments prey to decay and to vandals once the cemetery closed for good in 1975. Happily, help was at hand in the shape of the Friends of Highgate Cemetery and today the site is being returned to its former state by a knowledgeable band of volunteers who, though controversially still charging visitors to come in, are also on hand to provide detailed and fascinating guided tours of one of Victorian London's most evocative and extraordinary hidden landscapes.

OLD OPERATING THEATRE

ST THOMAS STREET, SE1

As a reminder of our mortality, there's little to beat the grisly horrors of early surgery and in London nowhere better to get a feel for it than in the shadow of Southwark Cathedral, at 9a St Thomas Street. Somewhat surprisingly given its location behind Guy's Hospital, London's oldest surviving operating theatre was originally a part of St Thomas's Hospital. This had been founded close by as early as 1106, probably within the Priory of St Mary Overie. In 1862, however, its original site was cleared to make way for London Bridge station and the hospital was rebuilt on the river at Lambeth Palace Road (to a design approved by Florence Nightingale, who had established a school of nursing there).

Before the move the hospital had contained two different operating theatres, one for male patients and this one for females. It had been constructed in the attic of what had once been the parish church of St Thomas, before this had been remodelled as the Chapter House for the nearby cathedral. The same space had also at one point served as an apothecary's herb garret and, incredibly, once the hospital was moved upstream it remained completely hidden from view until as recently as 1956. By that time it had been empty and bricked up for nearly a hundred years, but careful research – and generous funding from the medical charity the Wolfson Foundation – has enabled the theatre's trustees to effect an accurate and wholly authentic restoration of this gruesome space.

Part of its grisliness relies on its date. As the only surviving remnant of the original hospital, and completed in 1821, it can thus be said to precede by a good decade or more the long-overdue arrival of the happy oblivion that is ether and chloroform. It is true that London was said by Thomas Beddoes (1760–1808) in the nineteenth century to be 'the best spot . . . probably in the whole world where Medicine can be taught as well as cultivated to best advantage'. But looking round the little theatre now, with its five tiers of standings from which students were able to observe the master surgeons at work, the overwhelming sense is still one of mounting terror.

Far removed from the usual view of Georgian society with its elegant architecture, busy coffee houses and powdered noblemen trading sophisticated banter, here you glimpse a far less polite place. A place where heavily perspiring surgeons wearing blood-stained butchers' aprons cut away limbs and diseased flesh without anaesthetics, without antiseptics, and by our standards without any real idea about what it was that they were doing.

Admittedly, as a nod to these gentlemen's high ideals and the healing arts, a sign on the wall reads 'Miseratione non mercede' (Act out of compassion, not for gain). But the reality of the procedures undertaken probably had more to do with the box of sawdust beneath the operating table – put there to catch the blood – not to mention the small table to one side containing a selection of pliers, saws and other cutting instruments which would have looked more at home on a carpenter's bench or in the oily grip of an engineer.

SEVERNDROOG CASTLE

CASTLEWOOD PARK, SE18

For anyone with an eye for the odd or unusual, a journey to this corner of south-east London is a must. Not just to see the work of Vanbrugh, Nash, Wyatt and others on the Royal Regiment of Artillery's thrilling and architecturally diverse patch of Woolwich (q.v.) but also to visit one of London's biggest memorials – and its oldest surviving folly tower – the gloriously named Severndroog Castle which now hides among the trees of a public park on Shooter's Hill.

Built to commemorate the capture of Suvarnadrug off the coast of Malabar in the East Indies, this magnificently eccentric 60ft triangular tower also stands as a memorial to one William James, Bart, having been erected by his widow, Lady James of Eltham, the year after his death, from apoplexy, at his daughter's wedding in 1783.

Appointed to the command of the Honourable East India Company's strategically important Bombay Marine, it was (says a plaque affixed to the tower) 'this Gallant Officer's Atchievements [*sic*] . . . and superior Valour and able Conduct' which won the day in April 1755 when his frigate *Protector* turned her forty cannon against no fewer than four Angria pirate forts and a total of 134 enemy guns.

Of sufficiently humble birth to have run away to sea to escape punishment for poaching, James nevertheless returned to a genuine hero's welcome, receiving a baronetcy and eventually rising to the chairmanship of the Directors of the Honourable East India Company. All this in recognition of what the company's chronicler Robert Orme described as his 'spirited resolution [which] destroyed the timorous prejudices which had for twenty years been entertained of the impracticality of reducing any of Angria's fortified harbours'.

Even allowing for the apparent invincibility of Britain's imperial progress at this time, the destruction of Suvarnadrug/Severndroog was by all accounts never the expected outcome. It is fitting, then, that while the battle and its hero may have been largely written out of history, Lady James's grand monument survives to bear witness to this otherwise forgotten triumph.

Now more than a little scruffy (and unfortunately located close to the main road that the old Roman Watling Street has become), the tower with its three hexagonal corner turrets was designed in yellow stock brick by Richard Jupp. The Honourable East India Company surveyor, also responsible for Painshill Park in Surrey, here combined Georgian and Gothic features to leave us with one of the most refined and elegant prospect towers in the whole of the country.

Though denied access to the top these days, one imagines that even through the trees the view must be impressive given its height above sea level and above most of London. Certainly it was outstanding in 1786 when the tower was used as an observation point by a pre-Ordnance Survey mapmaker who recognised the usefulness of a stable platform 46ft higher than the cross on the top of St Paul's. In later years the castle became party to frivolity, becoming a popular venue for revels – complete with quadrilles danced to a select portion of the Woolwich Military Band, price 7s 6d to admit a lady and her gentleman and to include a cold collation, tea and coffee, wine, negus, mixed liquor et cetera. Perfectly delightful, but perhaps not quite what Lady James had in mind for her poor, dead, sweet William.

TRINITY HOSPITAL

HIGHBRIDGE, SE10

Something of a little wedding cake on the river – Lord Snowdon likened it to something Clough Williams-Ellis would have enjoyed at his Welsh fantasy village, Portmeirion – Trinity Hospital is the oldest surviving building in the centre of Greenwich. It had been founded by Henry Howard, 1st Earl of Northampton (1540–1614), the year before he died.

The builder of what came to be known as Northumberland House on the Strand, and according to the *Dictionary of National Biography* 'the most learned noble of his day', before settling upon this as a way of perpetuating his memory, Howard clearly enjoyed a life of danger and intrigue. Described by one Victorian biographer as 'a monster of wickedness and hypocrisy', he was imprisoned in the Fleet for publishing a work against judicial astrology and accused of treating with Spain. He was also heavily involved in the trial of Guy Fawkes (despite being a lifelong Catholic himself) and remains under suspicion of having connived in the slow poisoning of the poet Sir Thomas Overbury in the Tower.

His almshouses, however, with their chapel dedicated in 1617, are a far more attractive memorial to him and were intended to accommodate twenty poor pensioners. Supported by an annual income of £600, a dozen of these were to be local to Greenwich with a further eight coming from Shotesham St Mary in Norfolk. Shotesham was the village of Howard's birth, where he kept an estate as well as another hospital he had founded, and this explains the hospital's alternative name: Norfolk College.

Reordered and refaced in stucco in about 1815, the hospital survives and is now administered by the Mercers' Company. It occasionally opens its doors to the public and, despite the reworking, much of Howard's original structure survives. Not just staircases, but also the attractive cobbled courtyard and garden (through which passes the famous Greenwich Meridian), a courtroom and a panelled treasury. The chapel with its stupendous east window has been somewhat altered, however, but it still contains parts of the tomb of the founder, carved by Nicholas Stone. Brought here by the Mercers from Dover Castle – Howard was a sometime Warden of the Cinque Ports – it shows him kneeling on a cushion, in armour, and wearing the cloak of the Garter.

The address, Highbridge, was the site of a fifteenth-century bridge or embarkation point for the landing of goods and passengers. As such it is also thought to be the point beyond which, according to a decree passed in 1453 by the Venetian Senate, Venetian galleys were forbidden to proceed. Today, however, any romance of such an association is lost beneath the bulk of the adjacent power station, built in 1906 to provide the electricity required by London's trams.

WHITTINGTON COLLEGE

COLLEGE HILL, EC4

When Richard Whittington died childless in 1423, after serving as Lord Mayor on four separate occasions, his executors were charged with the foundation of a college of priests to say masses for the souls of Whittington, his wife and Richard II (1367–1400). To this end a charter was quickly obtained from Henry VI, paving the way for the College as well as an almshouse, the two to be known collectively as Whittington College and to be associated with the nearby church of St Michael Paternoster Royal.

Deriving its name from Riole, an adjacent street which since the thirteenth century had been popular with merchants importing wines from La Reole in the region of Bordeaux, in 1409 the church had been rebuilt by Whittington who lived next door and was to be interred there a decade and a half later.

Prior to this St Michael Paternoster had been an archiepiscopal peculiar, but the executors of Whittington's estate obtained the necessary permissions from Canterbury and the College soon became home to five priests and a master, required to speed the passage of their benefactor's soul to Heaven. However, dedicated to the Holy Ghost and the Virgin Mary, and with its best-known master the celebrated Lollard and heretic Reginald Pecock, the College was suppressed in 1548 and its buildings sold off for the not insubstantial sum of £92.

The almshouse, meanwhile, was to enjoy something of a peripatetic existence. Intended for twelve poor men and a tutor, it was originally housed in a new building between the College and the church. Later it was removed to Highgate Hill, and then to Felbridge in Sussex where it is still run today under the auspices of the Mercers' Company. Funding it using income from Whittington's City estate, and this nearly 600 years after his death, the Mercers also took the original buildings to accommodate their own school.

In time, the name Whittington College became attached to another such institution, a pretty little row of Gothic Revival almshouses in Islington, but this was later demolished by the local council as part of a road-widening scheme. As a result, and with Whittington's tomb at first plundered and then lost, although a mummified cat was found in the church in 1949, the original foundation survives today only in the name of this narrow thoroughfare and in its spectacular stone gateway.

That said, with its richly decorated, late seventeenth-century pediments and, behind the left-hand archway, a small but charming courtyard, the gatehouse has not completely lost its previous associations. In fact, in more recent years part of it was converted into Whittington's Wine Bar, thus in a sense honouring both the man and the longstanding connection between the wine trade and this particular City ward: Vintry, i.e. *Vintarii* or wine importers.

'It is not what they built, it is what they knocked down'

James Fenton,
German Requiem,
1981

4
MONUMENT ALLEY
Folies de Grandeur

CALEDONIAN MARKET TOWER

CLOCK TOWER PLACE, N7

Incredibly, cattle were still being driven into the City, and slaughtered there, until 1855. It was only then, after nearly 700 years of such messy activity, that the City Corporation finally took heed of complaints about blood running down the streets around Smithfield (and entrails being dumped in the drains) and transferred the trading of live cattle and horses to its new Metropolitan Cattle Market in Islington.

In fact the giant 30-acre site had already been developed, by an independent entrepreneur called John Perkins. But after some horse-trading, as it were, his enterprise was eventually taken over by the Corporation, its new market being opened by the Prince Consort on 13 June 1855. After that livestock – as many as 50,000 cattle, sheep and pigs at a time – were brought here to be sold every Monday, Thursday and Friday.

On the days in between, a general market grew up on the site with, on occasion, more than 2,000 different traders and pedlars setting up their stalls in the empty animal pens. They came here to trade literally anything for which they could find a buyer. In the main that meant mostly worthless bric-a-brac but not infrequently stolen goods too – in the 1920s it was reported that one punter picked up a long string of rare black pearls for just 7s 6d – so it was perhaps unsurprising that the site was cleared for redevelopment after the Second World War and the tinkers told to be on their way.

The more legitimate dealers among them relocated to Bermondsey Street – hence the famous antique market's current name: the New Caledonian Market – and by the mid-1960s housing covered much of the Islington site. Happily, however, some traces of the old market survive, including the original iron railings in Market Road, three of the four taverns which once marked the boundary, and best of all the imposing clock tower and carillon which formed the centrepiece of the market until it closed in 1939. Designed by J.B. Bunning who had just completed nearby Holloway Prison, it was built on the site of Copenhagen House. This had been a tea garden based around a gabled seventeenth-century house, a place which derived its name from the fact that a Danish prince or ambassador was thought to have sheltered there during the Great Plague of 1665.

Amid some opposition the tea garden had been swept away in 1853 and in its place Bunning built this wonderfully jolly white stone tower. However, being everything that his Holloway was not – bright, exuberant, cheerfully Italianate – its solid rather than soaring arched buttresses today stand somewhat forlornly above a council playing field surrounded by uninspiring developments from the 1960s and '70s.

COLCUTT TOWER

IMPERIAL INSTITUTE ROAD, SW7

As if it were not enough of a paradox that, at nearly 300ft, London's tallest folly manages to keep a low profile – passers-by generally fail to notice it, and even the locals don't seem to know quite where it is – the fact that the tower is in the middle of South Kensington rather than in some distant suburb serves only to compound the mystery of its almost total anonymity. That said, the very fact that this is such a densely populated area is of course what keeps Colcutt Tower so well hidden from view. Even at 287ft it somehow manages to disappear among the more recent, much lower additions to Sir Aston Webb's Imperial College. At least it does until one gazes back in that direction from the open spaces of Hyde Park and Kensington Gardens and sees it for what it is: by far the tallest building in this part of London.

Also known as the Queen's Tower – its completion was always intended to mark Victoria's first fifty years on the throne – what we see today is all that remains of the impressive-sounding Imperial Institute which had been founded after the Colonial Exhibition in 1886.

Originally T.E. Colcutt – best known as the author of the Savoy Hotel, Simpson's-in-the-Strand and the visually exuberant Palace Theatre – designed three of these immense Renaissance-style towers with their distinctive copper roofs. Of these only one is still in existence, having had its base and foundations considerably reinforced in order that it could survive being free standing.

It nearly didn't survive, mind you, as there were plans to demolish it in the 1960s. Despite the evident quality of Colcutt's architecture (and the very real majesty of his 704ft façade stretching the length of Imperial Institute Road), the Institute proved surplus to requirements and was gradually cleared away, in stages, to make room for the rapidly expanding Imperial College. Happily, sufficient supporters were found to mount a campaign for this last piece, however, and after much debate the lofty tower was allowed to live on.

Colcutt also devised other schemes to further aggrandise the capital, perhaps the most outstanding being a design he unveiled in 1906 for a new Charing Cross road bridge. Drawing inspiration from the old London Bridge and clearly Florence's medieval Ponte Vecchio, Colcutt designed a bridge with fifty shops on each side of the roadway, the rows sheltering behind twin classical colonnades. The bridge itself lined up along an axis stretching from a relocated Waterloo station to Trafalgar Square, and he wanted it to terminate at its northern end with an obelisk erected where Craven Street meets Northumberland Avenue.

It would have been magnificent, but alas was never to be. Instead we have just the tower where, on royal anniversaries, a number of bells named after Queen Victoria and her children still ring from the top of the tower. Perhaps that's when the locals look up and wonder where the sound is coming from, but for the rest of the year Colcutt's great handsome folly eases back into undeserved obscurity.

COWFORD LODGE

BUCKINGHAM PALACE, SW1

The tiny gate lodge to Ely Place may be even smaller, and the porter's lodge at Middle Temple more ornate in its choice of details, but neither matches the sheer monumentality of Cowford Lodge nor, it has to be said, its utter uselessness, since both of those two are at least still able to perform something akin to their original function. Cowford Lodge, diagonally opposite Buckingham Palace, remains a complete mystery. Even the name is made up, having been conferred on it less than ten years ago by the Earl of Snowdon who picked this one after identifying a nearby crossing point on one of London's 'lost' rivers, the Tyburn.

It is, however, at least known to date from about 1911 or 1912. That was the time when, fresh from completing the initial stages of his imposing and quite radical scheme for the University of Birmingham, RIBA president Aston Webb was busily reordering the Mall. Installing Admiralty Arch at one end and re-facing the Palace at the other using the same Portland stone we see here, Webb was later knighted and became only the second architect ever to be appointed to the presidency of the Royal Academy.

Compact yet massive, impressively monolithic yet somehow apparently invisible to passers-by, it makes little sense as an actual lodge for it is in the wrong position. Any guard function seems similarly unlikely for it is just as clearly in the wrong place for a sentry box. Instead, today, much like the little rustic cottage at the centre of Soho Square (q.v.) and the small French *fabriques* in Grosvenor Gardens, it is used simply for storing hosepipes and spades.

It has been suggested that it might once have been a police post, and this in turn has prompted conspiracy theorists to propose a more sinister alternative – namely that the lodge is actually some kind of subsidiary portal into the hidden network of secret access and escape tunnels, long rumoured to connect the Palace to various government buildings and transport hubs. Seems unlikely, but it is an appealing thought.

THE PIRATE CASTLE

OVAL ROAD, NW1

Somewhat dubiously described by its young members as the last fortified building to have been constructed in Britain, the Pirate Castle in Camden owes its name to a waterside youth club. This had been founded in the mid-1960s by Jestyn Reginald Austen Plantagenet Phillips, otherwise the 2nd Viscount St Davids, Old Etonian and a lieutenant in the Royal Naval Voluntary Reserve.

Its first home had been in the founder's garden which backed on to the Regent's Canal, the members becoming somewhat infamous on this stretch of the water for mounting 'rattling-tin raids' on any passing canal boats (hence the pirate soubriquet). Their objective was to raise money to fund the building of a proper clubhouse to replace the old Grand Union barge *Rosedale* which had more recently been pressed into service to provide accommodation. Through these raids and other initiatives they eventually reached their target a decade later, and finally in 1977 moved into this compact but chunky castle which had been designed for them by one of London's most prolific architects, Colonel Richard Seifert.

Located close to the top of Camden's flight of three locks, with its twin across the water serving as a a pumping station supplying coolant to the high-voltage cables running under the towpath, it was officially opened by the Lord Mayor of London. In traditional pirate fashion he was then held in the dungeon – actually the club's boat deck – until a suitable ransom was paid.

These days the Pirate Castle is available for hire for children's parties and so on, but it is primarily still associated with messing about in boats – canoes and rowboats as well as barges – and over the years thousands of young Londoners have come here for an early introduction to what must still be, after nearly 200 years, London's least-known transport network.

And as such it is well located, for there is plenty to see on this metropolitan section of the Grand Union Canal once you get out on the water. As well as affording one a highly unusual duck's-eye view of London Zoo, there is at one end the Maida Vale tunnel where once bargees were required to 'walk' their vessels. This meant covering some 270 yards through the darkness, crew members lying on the roof on their backs while the horse was led through the streets above. Further downstream the Islington Tunnel is longer still, at nearly 1,000 yards, although as early as 1826 a steam tug was here provided to haul the vessels half a mile under the streets of London. Pulling its way on a chain lying on the canal bed, this remained in use until the late 1920s.

The strangest thing on this section, however, is probably Macclesfield Bridge. One of more than forty bridges over the Regent's Canal, like many on Britain's canal network its support pillars – in this case made of cast iron – have grooves in them, worn over the centuries by tow-ropes from the days of real horse-power. Curiously, though, these are on the wrong, i.e. the landward, side, the pillars having been turned round (to balance up the wear) when the bridge was rebuilt after a catastrophic explosion on board the gunpowder barge *Tilbury* in 1874. The same explosion wrecked the house of painter Lawrence Alma-Tadema, and enabled several animals to make their escape from the Zoo.

PORT OF LONDON AUTHORITY

TOWER HILL, EC3

Hugely impressive, typically and confidently Edwardian, unforgiveably bombastic or, as one architectural historian put it, simply a case of baroque gone berserk, the Port of London Authority's monumental temple to imperial greatness can at least be said to stand up to the Tower of London which might otherwise completely dominate this busy traffic intersection in the middle of London.

To be fair, at the time Sir Edwin Cooper built it (1912–22), the PLA was an authentic, major world power. The result of the long overdue amalgamation of the various competing dock companies which for several centuries prior to 1909 had run and regulated the hugely important Port of London, it had responsibility for a 70-mile stretch of water from Teddington to the Nore lightship and exercised almost total control over what was by far the largest complex of docks in the entire world.

What Nikolaus Pevsner likened to 'a super-palace for an international exhibition, showy, happily vulgar', it was opened by Lloyd George – his last public act as prime minister – as an enduring monument to Edwardian optimism. The sort of optimism, that is, which in less than thirty years saw the PLA construct 80 acres of new deepwater docks and more than 6 miles of quayside while dredging a channel 1,000 yards wide and an incredible 50 miles long in order to give the largest commercial ships access to the very heart of London and the British Empire.

Commissioning new equipment and machinery costing some £20 million over the same period, and raising the total annual tonnage handled from 40 to over 60 million, the Authority can perhaps be forgiven a certain amount of self-congratulation. Forgiven too for the destruction of the many small courts and alleyways which were swept away to make room for this behemoth, even if today the building which replaced them looks somewhat elephantine alongside the graceful elegance of the nearby Georgian Trinity House.

Now standing on its own private island enclosed by the latter's Trinity Square, Seething Lane and Pepys and Muscovy Streets, it is not just the sheer bulk of the PLA's compass-aligned central tower which makes such an impact. It is also its extraordinarily intricate detailing which includes some very weird iconography – in the City the bulls might make sense, if only there were bears as well – together with some massive statues of suitably nautical subjects.

Inside, nearly 200,000sq. ft of offices are grouped around a lofty central hall, 110ft in diameter and nearly 70ft tall. But just as new uses have had to be found for the docks themselves, so the Authority itself has withdrawn to more modest premises, leaving behind it this mighty edifice as a reminder of happier or at least more influential times when this corner of London was the very epicentre of global trade.

ST ANTHOLIN'S SPIRE

ROUND HILL, SE26

Even in an age when the delights of architectural salvage are well understood, one is still surprised to discover the reasonably well-preserved spire of a genuine Wren church tower in the middle of a local authority housing estate. Particularly so when the fragment in question is historically as significant as this piece of the Watling Street church of 1678, which had originally been dedicated to St Anthony the Hermit.

Of course there are plenty of other London churches and parts of churches which have migrated. For example, All Hallows Grass Church, which was first mentioned as early as 1053 and was also the last church to be rebuilt by Wren after the Great Fire in 1666: when its tower was deemed unsafe in 1939 it was duly removed from Lombard Street to north Twickenham (along with the porch from the former Priory of St John at Clerkenwell). Similarly, after sustaining bomb damage a couple of years later, the ruins of the church of St Mary the Virgin in Aldermanbury were eventually shipped to Fulton, Missouri, and rebuilt as a memorial to Sir Winston Churchill.

The fate of this one is far sadder, though. Not just because St Antholin's was considered one of Wren's finest designs, but also because the spire has come to rest in such unprepossessing surroundings. The actual destruction took place in 1875 and was intended to clear a way through the Ward of Cordwainer for the new Queen Victoria Street. What remained of the site was quickly sold for development – the £44,990 thus realised being used for a new, less distinguished St Antholin's in Nunhead Lane, Peckham – and with the octagonal spire now redundant, it was sold for just a fiver to Robert Harrild who erected it here, on a red brick plinth, in the garden of his Round Hill House.

As a piece of garden statuary it probably looked rather good. However, with the garden gone the way of the church, and the house but a distant memory, St Antholin's spire really does deserve a better resting place than the one it has now.

SHRI SWAMINARAYAN TEMPLE

BRENTFIELD ROAD, NW10

The eighteenth-century Spanish and Portuguese synagogue in Bevis Marks is one of the City's most unexpected treasures. The Peace Pagoda lends some elegant sophistication to the Battersea river bank and the Russian Orthodox cathedral beneath the Chiswick flyover is one of west London's most incongruous sights. None, however, comes even close to rivalling the impact or almost hallucinogenic qualities of Neasden's sensational Shri Swaminarayan Temple.

Built by Hindu volunteers, its construction absorbed many thousands of tons of fine Italian marble, of Bulgarian grey limestone and of solid teak. In a large part this was funded by the proceeds of one of the largest drinks-can recycling schemes ever run in the UK, and all of the materials were first shipped to India to be carved, numbered and finished by more than 1,500 sculptors. The end result, with its intricately stepped spires and gleaming white finish, could not provide a more enthralling sight against the backdrop of Wembley Stadium – the new one or the old – which looms on the horizon nearly everywhere you go in this dreary part of London.

The contrast between the two is not just in their appearance either, but also in the manner of their original conception. An authentically spiritual enterprise where the football ground is wholly commercial, the temple was supported from the start not by big business and sponsorship, but rather by individuals and genuine enthusiasm. Similarly, while the new Wembley merely trumpets the latest trends in silicon-chip-inspired new technology, the temple (which has been likened to the very best sort of cappuccino foam made solid) is a real celebration of traditional craftsmanship and skills.

Unsurprisingly the largest temple of its kind anywhere outside India (also the first building in this style to have been built anywhere in the world for more than a century), it has had a remarkable effect on its immediate surroundings. The local Hindu community obviously love it and are justifiably proud of what they and their families have achieved here. But it makes a huge impact on visitors too, not just the tourists who seek it out but the accidental ones as well. Like the north country delivery driver who, after losing his way once he came off the nearby North Circular, told the *Guardian* newspaper, 'the spirit in which it is being built . . . I was just gob-smacked. It was like . . . I don't know. I've been back four times just to watch this . . . You want to touch it, breathe it in.'

Certainly you do, not only because of its genuinely cathedral-like scale – complete with a surrounding moat the whole *Mandir* is more than 70ft tall, nearly 200ft long and covers an acre and a half – but also its exuberance and the complexity of its decorated domes and cheerfully rococo pinnacles which tower over the red-tiled architecture of flat, grey and conventional postwar London.

It is about as far from English taste as one could possibly get – a welcome departure from 'traditional' Anglo-Indian architecture which historically has been restricted to follies, aristocratic tea houses and seaside pavilions for extravagant prince regents. More than anything the temple is a pleasing reversal of a well-established pattern: where once the English scattered the sub-continent with second-rate Gothic churches and classical palaces full of bureaucrats, Britain's Indian community is now confidently returning the compliment – in a manner that celebrates the heavens and is clearly not afraid to make itself felt.

SPENCER WELL-HOUSE

ARTHUR ROAD, SW19

Among London's many odd if delightful bye-laws is the one obliging every golfer on Wimbledon Common to wear a pillar-box red outer garment, a requirement which dates back to 1865 when Earl Spencer first gave leave to some officers of the London Scottish Rifle Regiment to lay out a golf course on his land.

The Spencers were lords of the Manor of Wimbledon until a few years ago when, to the dismay of many locals, the present earl sold the title (together with three other similarly minor ones it raised US$336,000). This particular title descended from the Hon. John Spencer – later the first earl – who had inherited it with some property from Sarah, Duchess of Marlborough, in her will of 1744.

To replace the dowager's house (which had been designed for her by the Earl of Pembroke but burned down in 1785), John's son, George John, had Henry Holland build him a new one. This survived on Arthur Road until as late as 1949, but clearly the fate of the original house worried him since,

> for the preservation of his noble manor-house at Wimbledon against fire, and to be well supplied with water [he] ordered a well to be dug at some distance from the house, to the amazing depth of near 600 feet; it was begun on the 31st of May 1798, and on Saturday, the man who was first employed upon the undertaking, gave the signal to the person above to draw him up, as he had found a spring, and was immersed in water so deep that his life became endangered.
>
> This was at eleven o'clock in the morning, and at three in the afternoon the fluid rose to 350 feet: and during Sunday and yesterday, its increase was more than a foot an hour; the water, proceeding from a rock, is remarkably sweet; and from the strata it passes through, is strongly impregnated with mineralic qualities. This valuable concern has already cost his lordship two thousand pounds, but will fully recompense him by his utility; as, before this well was finished, the only supplies for the family were either rain falling . . . or water which the servants procured from the adjoining fishponds.

Built on the site of the duchess's stables, this new Wimbledon Park House was eventually sold to a developer in the 1840s after which (while fragments of the Capability Brown park which surrounded it survive) it was gradually overcome by the development of the nearby streets. Today, as a result, not much of it remains. Near the church there is a stuccoed lodge of the early nineteenth century marking the former entrance; otherwise there is just this, the earl's great octagonal well-house. With the former recesses beneath its immense dome converted to windows, it was remodelled into a distinctive and historic private home in 1975.

STOKE NEWINGTON PUMPING STATION

GREEN LANES, N4

Even now one is surprised to discover a grim French (or possibly Scottish) medieval castle standing 200ft tall amid the mock-Tudor semis of north London suburbia. Surprised as well to learn that it is not the former dream-home of a megalomaniac with medieval pretensions but rather a Victorian pumping station designed to move clean water into the capital rather than sewage out of it. Then again, the lengths to which Victorians would go to disguise such things are perhaps no more extreme than those to which the modern Londoner will go to keep fit, and certainly building a bogus castle of this sort is arguably no more bizarre than the notion of 'indoor mountaineering', which is what William Chadwell Mylne's forbidding structure has been used for since 1995.

Mylne completed it in 1856 as part of the New River scheme, a project which was designed to bring fresh water into London in the wake of yet another cholera epidemic. The New River had had its origins in the early seventeenth century when Sir Hugh Myddleton, royal jeweller and wealthy entrepreneur, set out to channel water nearly 40 miles from Great Amwell in Hertfordshire to a spot near Sadler's Wells. Unfortunately by 1850 the grand plan was in trouble.

By then its sources were being condemned as impure, and the channel itself was clearly being used as a dumping ground for all manner of vegetable, animal and even human waste. At the same time the gravity fall into London had become so gentle that, as reported in a paper entitled *A Microscopic Examination of the Water Supplies to the Inhabitants of London*, it favoured 'the development of the lower forms of animal and vegetable life'. Accordingly new filtration works were commissioned for which Mylne – eighth in line in a remarkable nine-generation dynasty of master masons and architects stretching back to sixteenth-century Dundee – conceived the Stoke Newington Pumping Station to pump an incredible one million gallons of clean water every day.

Perhaps with a confidence born of nearly forty-five years' service as surveyor and engineer to the New River Company – not to mention the fact that the post had previously been held by his father and was by now semi-hereditary – he became a bit carried away. Basing his designs on Stirling Castle (so he said), Mylne created something truly formidable, built around a robustly styled 'keep' to house six giant steam engines, with immense buttresses to conceal their flywheels and no fewer than three mighty towers. The tallest of these was actually the boiler-house chimney, while another with an immense square top was designed to accommodate the water tank.

He stopped short of digging a moat, maybe guessing that it too would provide a breeding ground for those lower life forms. He succeeded in giving his castle an authentically impregnable air, however, mostly by siting it on a raised mound whose exaggerated contours made it the equal of anything one might find in a medieval illustrated text.

A century later, though, technology caught up with the castle, redundancy loomed and this incredible landmark found itself on English Heritage's Buildings at Risk Register. For such a giant there seemed little hope of rescue, at least until 1993 when a small group of enthusiasts conceived a new use for it and raised the necessary capital to buy a lease. They next commissioned Nicholas Grimshaw and Partners to convert it into an indoor climbing arena and, barely two years later, found themselves with a maze of different artificial rock faces. Today trainee mountaineers can lay siege to the castle once more, albeit from within rather than without, while climbing over Mylne's original brick arches and his massive cast-iron columns in a controlled, weatherproof and quite delightfully imaginative environment.

Temple Bar

Paternoster Square, EC4

It was the Romans who first built a wall around the City (c. AD 200), 3 miles long and enclosing approximately 330 acres, and although sections of the wall have survived the intervening centuries seven gates sadly have not. While their original locations can be gleaned from the naming of nearby streets, Ludgate, Newgate, Aldgate, Aldersgate, Cripplegate, Moorgate and Bishopsgate all disappeared in the 1760s. But one other – Temple Bar – has now returned to the capital, after more than 125 years away.

Popularly supposed to have been designed by Sir Christopher Wren – although, in the absence of any documentation to support this, some architectural historians credit the mason instead – Joshua Marshall's great Portland stone edifice of 1672 was originally erected in Fleet Street on the orders of Charles II. It was conceived as a grand western entrance into the City. Above the main carriage arch (there were two smaller ones for pedestrians) were placed matching statues by John Bushnell of Charles I and Charles II facing westwards, with similar statues of James I and Anne of Denmark in the corresponding niches on the other side. In the way of these things the Bar also proved a convenient place to display the bloody heads of any unfortunates careless enough to be caught and executed. These included the Rye House plotters – at which time telescopes could be hired for ½d to get a closer look at the spikes – among them Sir Thomas Armstrong, whose body parts were first boiled in brine to prevent them being eaten by birds.

In 1806 such grisly practices had fortunately ceased and the entire structure was then covered in black velvet for the funeral of Lord Nelson. But by 1870 Temple Bar had become a traffic bottleneck, whereupon it was swiftly dismantled and the more than 2,500 stones (weighing nearly 400 tons) stored in a yard off Farringdon Road. Eventually these caught the eye of one Lady Meux, Valerie Susie – variously described as a banjo-playing barmaid and an actress – who, having married into the junior ranks of the 'beerage', was looking for a suitable entrance to the Hertfordshire estate of her wealthy husband, Sir Henry Brent Meux.

The spot where it once stood was then marked by a representation of a griffin, the City's unofficial badge, denoting not just the western limit of the City but also the place where the monarch must stop and hand the sword of state to the Lord Mayor before proceeding into the City. The arch, meanwhile, was to all intents forgotten – at least by Londoners, although it remained an intriguing conversation piece in rural Hertfordshire. A century later, however, the crumbling arch – extended, centrally heated even, abandoned and, finally, shamefully neglected – became the subject of a campaign to have it removed from Theobalds Park and returned to the City.

That was in 1984 but in the event, the wheels of recovery and conservation grinding exceeding slow, it wasn't until 10 November 2004 that Temple Bar finally came home. After a remarkable £4 million restoration, all of it met by City funds, it was officially reopened by the Lord Mayor on its new site in the radically redeveloped Paternoster Square.

YORK WATERGATE

WATERGATE WALK, WC2

Now stranded 150 yards inland, and separated from the water not just by Embankment Gardens but also by a queue of traffic at least four cars deep, one now has only to stand by York Watergate to get a measure of Sir Joseph Bazalgette's incredible achievements. This is because when Charles Dickens lived nearby at 15 Buckingham Street – a dwelling which had earlier been occupied by Peter the Great and then Henry Fielding – the Thames would have washed right up against the base of the gate which had been built as the ceremonial river entrance to the gardens of the Duke of Buckingham's splendid York House.

Bazalgette changed all that, however, confining the tidal river with a series of great embankments – Victoria, Albert and Chelsea. In the process he created 52 acres of new central London with space beneath the roadways for service pipes, his new low-level sewers, wide tunnels for what was to become the District and Circle Lines, even a pioneering pneumatic railway to run underneath the Thames (although this last was never built). Looking at his work today, it is difficult, if not impossible, to get an accurate impression of what would have been there before, to understand indeed why the Strand was so named. It is similarly hard to credit, as the traffic pushes its way noisily along the busy A3211, that having originally been a footpath or bridle path along the river, for nearly 400 years it would have been one of the best addresses in England.

Ideally situated between Commerce and the Crown, between the cities of London and Westminster, it was here from about 1200 that a series of palaces sprang up. These included John of Gaunt's Savoy Palace, Durham House (which for a time was home to Simon de Montfort) and numerous 'inns' for the powerful abbots of Tewkesbury, Faversham and Winchcombe and for the bishops of Carlisle, Durham and Norwich. The churchmen were in time followed by noblemen, among them George Villiers, Duke of Buckingham, a favourite of James I who took over the former lodgings of the bishops of Norwich, although he preferred to live in Whitehall, using his historic riverside mansion merely as a place to entertain.

By 1670, however, the property speculators had moved in and this stretch of the river bank was heavily redeveloped by the likes of Nicholas Barbon. Today as a result there is little left: just the Savoy Chapel, still a personal possession of the monarch, the inevitable street names – because the Duke of Buckingham insisted every part of his name be commemorated there was once an Of Alley here as well as a Duke, George, Villiers and Buckingham Street – and of course the Watergate, dating back to 1626.

Better known for tombs and funerary monuments, it was built by Nicholas Stone. Its designer remains a mystery, however, with different authorities ascribing the Watergate to the builder himself, to Inigo Jones – this was very much the eighteenth-century view – and to Sir Balthasar Gerbier who was in the Duke's service at this time and was said to have modelled it on the Fontaine de Medicis in Paris' Luxembourg Garden. Whoever was responsible, it is a striking piece, highlighting the Villiers' arms and motto – *'Fidei coticula crux'* (the touchstone of Faith is the cross) – with the two lions' shields sporting anchors, symbolising the Duke's service as Lord High Admiral and Warden of the Cinque Ports.

‘ **There is nothing which has**

yet been contrived by man,

by which so much happiness

is produced as by a good

tavern or inn ’

James Boswell,
The Life of Samuel Johnson,
1791

5
MEET MINE HOST
Restaurants & Public Houses

THE BLACK FRIAR

QUEEN VICTORIA STREET, EC4

Compressed into the elbow of this area's busiest, messiest junction of road, rail and river, there is little if anything about the noisy approach to the wedge-shaped Black Friar to suggest one is about to enter such a glorious temple to England's Arts and Crafts Movement. It's true that high up on the building's apex there is the jolly friar himself, his statue stuck above a wide band of mosaic like the figurehead of an old galleon. But while he beams down at passers-by, in the nature of passers-by in London, they mostly keep their eyes firmly locked on the pavement and don't notice his welcoming smile.

For anyone who does glance up, however, it is clear the building of 1875 is a charmer. There is a pleasing economy in the way it has been squeezed on to such a small, unpromising scrap of land. It also has for modern London an unusual and attractive feature in the mosaic and metalwork band which spells out its name, derived from an adjacent Dominican foundation (only a tiny fragment of which now survives, in Ireland Yard).

It is the later interior of 1905, however, which really sets this place apart, a cheerful riot of creamy, rich-veined marble walls, barrel-vaulted ceilings and archways by H. Fuller Clarke. With hand-beaten Arts and Crafts copper murals and myriad little sculptures by Henry Poole, the theme is monkish but amusing, with friezes depicting yet more bucolic friars enjoying themselves. There are also strange slogans, admonishments and bon mots let into the stonework: 'Finery is Foolery' – 'Haste is Slow' – 'Seize Occasion' – 'Industry is All' – 'A Good Thing is Soon Snatched Up'.

The effect is deliberately busy, a bit camp but delightful. With gleaming gold leaf on the ceiling, cosy inglenooks with burnished brass firedogs and yet more warm, glowing copper, the Black Friar is also a place which manages to retain a pleasant sense of intimacy even when it is sufficiently crowded (and it frequently is) that drinkers are forced to spill out on to the pavement.

In the 1960s, with a certain sad inevitability, a group of speculators wished to unseat the Black Friar and develop his site. But thankfully for once the public outcry, led by Sir John Betjeman, was loud enough and listened to, and today a preservation order has secured what Nikolaus Pevsner describes as the capital's 'best pub in the Arts and Crafts fashion'.

That such an exuberant and unique building could have been lost seems incredible now, not least because with decor as golden and as grand in its way as the ersatz Louis XVI finery of the Ritz, the Black Friar remains one of London's most spectacular if informal dining rooms. Just as importantly, in an age of synthetic theming and the all-conquering gastro-pub, it has also somehow managed to retain the atmosphere of a proper London boozer: unfussy service, good beer and bangers and mash on the menu. You can even get a full roast for a fiver.

CABMEN'S SHELTER

ALBERT BRIDGE, SW3

Once upon a time there were more than sixty of them, but now fewer than a dozen of these large garden shed-like structures survive, each one still smart in its trademark green livery and dedicated to the cause of keeping cabbies from the bottle. The shelters' origins go back to 1874 when, attempting to hail a cab, Captain George Armstrong – late of the Indian Army and then managing editor of the *Globe* newspaper – found plenty of vacant vehicles on the stand but not a single driver for hire. Cabmen at this time, perhaps unsurprisingly, had a well-deserved reputation for hard drinking. Thus, on the evening in question, Armstrong eventually discovered a gaggle of them sheltering from the weather in a local tavern, trading occupational banter and availing themselves of the establishment's more obvious delights.

Together with several well-meaning philanthropists and propelled by typically Victorian good intentions, Captain Armstrong set out to devise a practical alternative, to find somewhere able to provide the same shelter and companionship as well as a cheap meal, but without the temptation of alcoholic liquor.

Edinburgh and Birmingham apparently had something similar already; however, Armstrong was thinking bigger, wishing to provide not just stoves on which to cook, and tables and benches, but also a selection of books and newspapers to read. (There were, however, to be strictures against discussing union business while inside.) For their part the Metropolitan Police decreed that, as the shelters were to occupy space on the Queen's Highway, each should be no larger than a horse and cab, and within a decade or so forty of them had been installed at a cost of approximately £200 apiece.

Maintained by the Cabmen's Shelters Fund, which through the Transport and General Workers Union was eventually empowered to collect a small levy from each of the drivers, they were an immediate success. Indeed, by 1894 the Fund secretary reported that the drivers were using them regularly and were 'extremely particular about their steaks . . . and everything of that kind and are as ready to complain as members of West End clubs if things are not right'.

As they were permitted to serve only cabbies, the club analogy was understandable, particularly by the 1920s when H.V. Morton was telling the story of 'The Junior Turf', a cabmen's shelter by Green Park which was ordered by Westminster Council either to desist from selling sausages to passers-by or to pay business rates like any other similarly commercial catering outlet. Unsurprisingly they opted for a return to their original exclusivity, although rumours persisted of white-tied toffs and even younger royals popping in for a late night bite on their way home from the '43' or the Embassy. Rumours abounded too of the explorer Sir Ernest Shackleton who, as one old cabbie told Morton, 'used to bring down great big books of photographs, and talk all night about his travels'.

More recently, however, improvements to the roadways have done for many shelters (just as the Luftwaffe did for several of them in the 1940s) and what with other changes in the way taxi drivers work their shifts around the capital it seems unlikely that the few remaining cabmen's shelters will survive much longer.

CIRO'S PIZZA
POMODORO
BISHOPSGATE CHURCHYARD, EC2

Said to have been modelled on a shrine forming part of the Church of the Holy Sepulchre in Jerusalem, this charming City curiosity was designed by G. Harold Elphick. He built it for Victorian entrepreneur James Forder and his brother, the structure intended to form the above-ground entrance for the Forders' extensive subterranean suite of luxurious Turkish baths. As its narrowness suggests, when it was completed in the 1890s it had to slot in between two nineteenth-century office buildings. A century later not much has changed in that, it being such an obviously low-rise structure in what is more than ever a high-rise environment, the pressure is clearly still on for its owners to resist more efficient utilisation of what must be an extremely expensive patch of land.

Although the Forders were among the bath-house industry's foremost players, the craze for what in Victorian times passed for an authentic Ottoman *haman* actually kicked off slightly earlier. The first of more than 600 Turkish baths in the British Isles had opened for business in cold, wet Ireland in the 1850s, offering visitors a sequence of luxuriously appointed and increasingly hot divans or cubicles interspersed with ice-cold showers.

This and its successors (including the Nevills' London chain of bath houses) differed from the genuine article in that the heat was 'dry', meaning the rooms were warmed by electric heaters rather than by the circulation of steam. This was because the Victorians believed that the higher temperature of electrical heat was likely to be more effective at relieving rheumatism and gout – a belief with which, as it happens, many experts now concur.

The baths having somehow survived the Blitz, the inevitable attempts at redevelopment and at least until the 1950s the steadily declining interest in Turkish baths as a whole, the brothers' original lease eventually expired and the building was converted into a restaurant. Appropriately for a while, as The Gallipoli and afterwards the Young Turks, it served Turkish food, later Indian when it was renamed the Sri India, but latterly, and most bizarrely, the only oriental building in the City now specialises in Italian pizza and pasta.

Unfortunately, as between times it was used as storage space, the majority of the building's fine fixtures and fittings are long gone. The winding staircase down to basement level with its faience tiles of tin-glazed earthenware, the cooling fountains of filtered water, the marble mosaic floors, the stained-glass windows and the choice of rose, douche, needle or spiral showers are all gone. Some of the tile work survives, however, the best of it being the 'Moorish' interlocking patterns which Elphick himself designed and had specially manufactured by Craven Dunnill at Jackfield in Shropshire's famous Ironbridge Gorge.

THE GRENADIER

WILTON ROW, SW1

This is arguably London's best-known haunted pub – and there are a few of those around. On one's first visit to the Grenadier with its famous sentry box it's hard to believe such a place really exists as the whole ensemble looks so much like a perfectly constructed set for a movie about London in the Swinging Sixties. Concealed round the bend in a tiny, hard-to-find mews just a couple of hundred yards from the hectic pell-mell of Hyde Park Corner, the Grenadier's secluded location provides the strongest possible contrast with the starchy and expensive formality of Belgravia proper. The truth though is that Wilton Row would have formed an integral part of Thomas Cubitt's master plan for the area, put there to service his and W.H. Seth-Smith's much grander terraces on Wilton Crescent.

Laid out between 1828 and 1830, when it was known as Crescent Mews, that fact alone puts paid to the most enduring myth about the place, namely that the tavern was originally built around the remains of a former officers' mess for the Palace guards. It also neatly scotches any idea that the Duke of Wellington might have dropped in from time to time to play a few hands with his junior officers. It's true he lived nearby at Apsley House, but he was notably ill-disposed towards both gambling and drinking in public. As a member of the Athenaeum, the 'Rag', the 'Senior', the City of London, the Oxford & Cambridge, Guards, Crockfords and several other clubs – with sixteen subscriptions only Lord Mountbatten seems to have belonged to more – it appears highly unlikely that a man of his standing would have chosen to patronise a common tavern.

Nonetheless, it is possible that some of the troops might have shared a pint here with chums in service in Wilton Crescent, that some of the younger officers might have gambled in the cellars and so possible too that one of their number could still be here in spirit having been inadvertently flogged to death after being discovered cheating at cards. Certainly the pub has plenty of military paraphernalia to lend the legend some credence, including a genuine bearskin – which is said in the past to have been groomed each week by a man from the nearby Wellington Barracks – as well as some nice old military prints and several cartoons and press cuttings about the pub and the ghost of the poor dead subaltern. His death, incidentally, is said to have occurred in September – this being the month when most of the 'disturbances' are reported by staff and customers alike.

KENSINGTON ROOF GARDENS

DERRY STREET, W8

Mature trees, splashing fountains, a pool, a stream, lawns, ducks and flamingos covering 1½ acres and all thriving nearly 100ft above one of the capital's busiest shopping streets, London's equivalent of Babylon's famous hanging gardens dates back to the 1930s and is the creation of department store magnate Trevor Bowen.

In 1936 Bowen commissioned Ralph Hancock, one of the leading landscape gardeners of the day, to create an extraordinary suite of three quite distinct gardens above Derry & Toms, the Kensington department store which had recently been acquired by his Barker's Stores group. The cost, some £25,000, was to include a classic, meandering English woodland garden to the south and, overlooking the High Street, a smaller Tudor and a more formal Spanish garden, the latter centred around an elegantly curved sun pavilion designed by Barker's own in-house architect, Bernard George.

As a feat of engineering it was quite something, with soil laid to a depth of 18ins over a drainage layer of brick and clinker and a vast waterproof membrane to protect the building beneath. This was then planted out with more than 500 different species of plants and shrubs – some of them arranged around rocks and boulders specially imported from Pennsylvania – the species being handpicked in order that each would be able to withstand the considerable pollution Hancock correctly surmised would be the bane of this uniquely extreme urban environment.

Thereafter 15,000 bulbs were purchased and planted each year, along with 38,000 bedding plants which were raised in the Roof Gardens' own rooftop nursery. Two years in the making, they were naturally a huge hit with shoppers. Even so, having first opened for business in the 1850s as a 'Toy & Fancy Repository', Derry & Toms was eventually taken over by House of Fraser and finally closed its doors in 1973 when this unique feature of the building was all but forgotten. Part of the store below was occupied by the short-lived but fondly remembered Biba enterprise, but it wasn't until 1981 that the Roof Gardens were taken over by the Virgin Group. By this time the local council had placed a Tree Preservation Order on several of the trees in order to preserve the Gardens' unique character.

Virgin now runs a successful nightclub in Bernard George's Sun Pavilion, as well as a restaurant, but allows the public the run of the gardens on those occasions when they are not being used for private or corporate functions. Arriving there via an ordinary lift in what now feels like a very conventional office building, the experience upon stepping out at the top is one not to be missed. Not just for the opportunity to explore the now gloriously mature gardens, with their immaculate lawns, palm trees and extremely pretty walks, but also for the chance to enjoy the genuinely panoramic views they afford over much of west London. Quite extraordinary.

OXO TOWER

BARGEHOUSE STREET, SE1

Amajor London landmark once more, now that the capital has at last started to make a bit more of its river, the Oxo Tower is presently best known as a restaurant but in its day must have been just about the most expensive and elaborate advertisement ever conceived. The tower's distinctive address dates back to a time when the safest and most comfortable way for a nobleman to travel to London from the royal precincts at Westminster was by water, this particular site having provided a convenient berth for the State Barge of James I. There being no need for such a thing during the Interregnum, under Oliver Cromwell it became a timberyard, although trade tokens found on the site more recently suggest that barges were still in use here until the late eighteenth century.

Parish records also indicate that the land was being used for butchery, a nice touch given what was to come, although by the end of the nineteenth century there was a power station here supplying electricity to the Post Office. In the 1920s this was taken over by the Leibig Extract of Meat Company which bought the site for £75,000.

In 1928 Leibig's directors planned to demolish most of the building but their architect Albert W. Moore retained and extended the river façade which he later described as 'the most pleasing and interesting of all the buildings along the South Bank'. Converting what was now known as Stamford Wharf into a mammoth cold-storage facility, Moore proposed spelling out his client's famous trademark in electric lights on a tall tower. However, he was refused permission by the London County Council, which at the time took a dim view of illuminated advertisements and other 'skysigns' above a certain height.

Planning what was to be the second highest commercial building in the capital, Moore's immediate response called for something he named 'elemental geometric forms', namely 10ft high windows fabricated by Crittall in Essex which clearly spelt out the word 'OXO' on all four sides of the tower. Something of a masterstroke, this arrangement enabled the company to broadcast its message day and night (and as far afield as Hampstead) while their dual function meant the branded signs could not technically be classified as advertisements.

In any event the finished structure with its attractive art deco detailing was by far the most attractive of the many wharves then crowding the southern bank, and calls for its destruction were ignored. Having cost a not inconsiderable £174,399 and eventually subsumed into the giant Vestey meat-packing empire, the warehouse continued to function as such for many years with a staggering 250 million sq. ft of storage space spread over nine floors. Meat was delivered by barge (as presumably it had been for 200 or 300 years) before being off-loaded using large cranes fixed on to the building and winched through the loading bays which can still be discerned on the river side.

By the early 1970s, however, the whole thing was largely derelict and an eyesore. Only a small part of Moore's structure was still being used – engaged in the production of so-called 'long eggs' destined for insertion into rectangular pork pies. Down below, two barges moored together on the water functioned as a floating helipad until 1984 when the site was rescued and redeveloped by the Coin Street Community Builders.

YE OLDE CHESHIRE CHEESE

FLEET STREET, EC4

It is an enduring but almost certainly false belief that Dr Johnson compiled his celebrated dictionary while consuming ale and biscuits in the City's most famous alehouse. Nevertheless, sitting in Ye Olde Cheshire Cheese, with its characterful gloom and sawdust-strewn wooden floors, it is not hard to picture the good doctor strolling here from his house in nearby Gough Square (q.v.), finding time to mull over a particularly tricky definition and whiling away the late hours with his friends.

Its entrance hidden away in Wine Office Court, a narrow alleyway off the main thoroughfare where once the city's winesellers came to obtain their warrants to trade, the present pub arose from the ashes of the Great Fire in 1667. But the cellars are evidently much older, incorporating part of the undercroft of a 600-year-old Carmelite monastery, as is the front step which, now protected by an iron guard, is worn thin by hundreds of years and thousands of feet.

The Central London chapel of the National Union of Journalists was formed here in 1907, and until very recently this warren of a place was still a favourite of writers and journalists. They and other regulars would have known it as 'The House', the tavern's given name being something of a red herring since the Cheshire in question was one Thomas Cheshire, whom records show as keeping the bar here in 1543.

Nearly four centuries on, one of his successors had a parrot that achieved a measure of celebrity when, in 1918, it fainted after mimicking 400 times a bottle of champagne popping open to celebrate the Armistice. The bird was also renowned for a vocabulary so blue and so extensive that when it died in 1926 aged forty the nascent BBC accorded it the unique honour of announcing its demise on the wireless.

Elsewhere at this living museum there is a useful board detailing the fifteen monarchs who have occupied the throne during the tavern's long history, and a grille through which can be glimpsed the dark waters of the Fleet river from which the street takes its name. Sadly, though, on the menu there is no longer any sign of 'Ye Pudding' for which the place was once well known. This weighed 50–80lb, took up to twenty hours to boil according to William Kent and had 'entombed therein beefsteaks, kidneys, oysters, larks, mushrooms and wondrous spices and gravies, the secret of which is known only to the compounder'. It was said at the time that the aroma on a breezy day reached as far as the Stock Exchange.

' **For a city consists in men, and not in walls nor in ships empty of men'**

Nicias,
in a speech to the
defeated Athenian army,
413 BC

6
CITY & GUILDS
The Liverymen

APOTHECARIES' HALL

BLACKFRIARS LANE, EC4

Somewhat surprisingly, given the value of even the smallest central London freeholds, thirty-eight livery halls still survive in the City – and one more if you include the Watermen and Lightermens' Hall on St Mary-at-Hill near Billingsgate, although this particular company, while established as early as the 1450s, has yet to be awarded its own livery. By far the most charming, however, is the Apothecaries' Hall, with its simple but elegant, stuccoed courtyard and thirteenth-century well. Built on land formerly owned by Lady Howard of Effingham (and before her the Dominican or Black Friars, who had a guest house on the site), it has been in the possession of the Worshipful Society of Apothecaries of London since 1632.

Responsible for two magical corners of the capital – the other being the similarly unexpected and delightful Chelsea Physic Garden – the society had received its original charter from James I a few years earlier. Already by then it had been in existence for a number of years, though originally as a part of the Grocers' Company until the increasing specialisation of its members led them to break away to form a separate entity in 1617.

From that date on their power and prestige grew rapidly, extending into areas formerly the preserve of barber-surgeons and physicians, so that by 1815 anyone passing the society's examinations was considered fully qualified for general practice in medicine. Indeed, even now, after nearly 400 years, the society is still very much involved in the education and examination of pharmacists, although it no longer plays a part in the physical retailing of drugs or medicines.

Past members of the society include Oliver Cromwell, John Keats and Sir Humphry Davy, the last two of whom would have known the present Hall since this was completely rebuilt between 1669 and 1671 by Thomas Locke after the Great Fire. Even so, traces can still be seen of the much older Dominican monastery in the medieval stonework underpinning the brick walls, an extraordinary thing when one considers that much of that building used even older materials, namely stone which the monks had salvaged from the Norman Castle Baynard.

The façade to the street, though, is more recent than Locke's work, although most of his building is still extant, including most obviously the Great Hall. With its splendid black oak panelling by Robert Burgys and Roger Davis, this houses an immense decorated chest donated to the society by William Clarke (one of the founding members) as well as a minstrels' gallery surmounted by the royal coat of arms. There is also at the foot of the main stairs a striking painting of Elizabeth I watching the defeat of the Armada – something which she is known not to have done – and in the Great Hall a seventeenth-century bust of Gideon de Laune, Anne of Denmark's apothecary, who is said to have fathered no fewer than thirty-seven children. The elaborate twenty-four-branch chandelier was presented to the society by its Master, Sir Benjamin Rawlings, in 1736.

ARMOURERS' HALL

81 COLEMAN STREET, EC2

The Worshipful Company of Armourers and Brasiers dates its foundation as far back as 1453, the year it received its first charter. However, a Guild of St George of the Armourers is known to have been in existence as early as 1322 and it was that body which originally leased the London Wall site on which the present hall stands. As later the company was to do, this guild sought from its earliest days to preserve a monopoly in the manufacture of armour and 'to maintain its dignity and quality'. This was achieved through a series of rigorous procedures controlling entry into apprenticeships and allowing for the inspection and hallmarking of all brass and copper goods, guns, armour and edged tools.

It was clearly therefore an organisation with very considerable powers by the time it erected its original hall on the site of 'The Dragon and two shoppes' in 1346. More than three centuries later, by which time the freehold had been purchased by the company, this building became one of very few City structures to survive the Great Fire. (It was stopped just a few yards away.) Many armourers with workshops in the surrounding alleys were less fortunate, however, although those rendered homeless were permitted by their fellow liverymen to conduct their trade from within the hall – providing they could do so without the use of either hammer or forge.

Notwithstanding this miraculous survival, the first hall was pulled down in 1795 to make way for a new one by William Cresswell. By this time the company had absorbed the Blacksmiths and later the Helmet Makers and Armour Repairers; perhaps the membership felt that the original building was now too small and insufficiently grand. However, in 1840 this too was swept away and replaced by the present late neo-Classical design by J.H. Good. Exactly 100 years later it was to survive yet another fire, when during the Blitz of 29 December 1940 a quick-thinking fireman broke in after spotting that the Court Room curtains were ablaze.

Architecturally it is a relatively modest building, lacking the appeal of the Apothecaries' and the glitter and Edwardian splendour of somewhere like the Drapers'. However, the decoration of its interior apartments still makes it one of the most spectacular, especially on dining-in nights when, with the tables laid for a banquet, candlelight from brass chandeliers is allowed to play not just on the silverware but on ranks of sixteenth- and seventeenth-century pikes, armour and assorted weaponry arranged around its high walls.

Among its other treasures is a painting, in the drawing room, of Anne Vavasour. As a Gentlewoman of the Queen's Bedchamber in 1580 she came to know Sir Henry Lee – one of only very few commoners at the time to get the Garter – who was Queen Elizabeth's Champion and later Master of the Royal Armouries. Before long she became Sir Henry's mistress, or as contemporary accounts put it (with commendable delicacy) his 'reading lady'.

FISHMONGERS' COMPANY

KING WILLIAM STREET, EC4

Active in London for more than 700 years, and with its hall on this site since 1434, the Fishmongers enjoy the dubious distinction of being the very first of forty livery companies to lose its building (along with a valuable collection of plate) to the Great Fire in 1666. First granted a charter by Edward I in 1272, the Fishmongers' original hall was built as early as 1310 and – reflecting their great prestige, derived from the religious importance of fish in the medieval diet – included a great hall, a counting house and a dwelling. In 1434, however, the current site was bequeathed to the company and a new hall of brick and timber was built on the river.

Among the first buildings to be completed after the fire, the majority of the work was credited to Edward Jarman, although Sir Christopher Wren is reported to have had a hand in it. (The two are known to have worked together on several projects.) With its distinctive twin flights of steps this structure can be seen in several views of the Thames by Canaletto; but sadly it too was swept away in 1827 to make way for Sir John Rennie's new London Bridge.

By then the company's power and influence were not what they had been. There were, for example, no more *leyhalmodes* held here, the peculiarly private courts of law at which all disputes relating to fish were adjudged by the Wardens regardless of whether they were between members of the company or between non-members (known as 'foreigners'). Nonetheless, a prestigious competition was held to determine who would design the new hall, the judging overseen by Sir Robert Smirke, the architect of the British Museum.

The winner, a bold Greek Revival design with discreet Soanian touches by Henry Roberts, was in marked contrast to the working men's cottages in Kennington he completed for Prince Albert (q.v.). The drawings themselves were drafted by one of his assistants, the young George Gilbert Scott, and the building was completed in 1834, since when it has remained more or less unaltered, despite sustaining some damage in the Blitz. Its chief glory is perhaps its magnificent riverside site – no other hall is so superbly situated – and the Thames façade is particularly grand, especially when viewed from the riverside walkway.

Despite further royal charters from successive monarchs, including Richard II, Henry V, Henry VI, Henry VII, Henry VIII, Edward VI, Mary, Elizabeth I and James I, the days are of course long gone when no fish could be sold in London except by the 'Mistery of the Fishmongers'. But as one of the Great Twelve Companies it retains some importance and influence within the City, not least because it is one of the very few old ones which still performs its original function. Thus, working fishmongers are even now represented among the nearly 300 liverymen, and all fish sold at Billingsgate are still required to be inspected by company officials known as Fishmeters.

A particularly proud possession of the Fishmongers' is the dagger on display in the hall with which a member, Sir William Walworth (d. 1385), broke the Peasants' Revolt by stabbing its leader Wat Tyler. In 1954 the Fishmongers commissioned Pietro Annigoni to paint his celebrated and much copied portrait of Queen Elizabeth II.

GOLDSMITHS' HALL

FOSTER LANE, EC2

With its eleven-bay façade, Goldsmiths' Hall is architecturally very much the equal of its near-contemporary, the Fishmongers', though it lacks that one's conspicuously impressive site. The company's fifth, it was designed by Philip Hardwick (1792–1870) and completed in 1835. Hardwick's client, the every-bit-as-grand-as-it-sounds Worshipful Company of Goldsmiths, had received its first charter in 1327, but records show a fraternity of goldsmiths active as early as 1180 and certainly by 1300 their wardens were marking articles of gold and silver with a leopard's head. Allocated the responsibility for the absolute purity of both metals (and more recently also platinum), the term 'hallmarking' thus derives from the ancient legal requirement for such objects to be brought to Goldsmiths' Hall for examination and assaying before they could be sold.

Very little is known of the fourteenth-century original, besides a foundation date of 1366 and that it had been home to the Bishop of London's brother, Nicholas de Segrave. This was rebuilt in 1407 by the splendidly named Sir Drue Barentyn, whose new building incorporated not just an Assay Office and secure vaults but also (wisely) an armoury and granary arranged around an inner courtyard. In his turn Nicholas Stone replaced this one in the early 1630s, his building being used as an exchequer by the Parliamentarians (1641–60) before being destroyed in the Great Fire and restored a year later by Edward Jarman.

By the 1820s, however, this was considered too old and inadequate, and was demolished to make way for the one we see today: an early English baroque design in Portland stone. Elements of Jarman's work survive – for example in the panelling in the Court Room – and naturally the hall contains an unrivalled collection of valuable plate which is occasionally available for public inspection.

The Goldsmiths also exercise perhaps the oldest responsibility of any of those companies which survive, as it plays an important role in the mysteriously named Trial of the Pyx. This is the occasion when the Queen's Remembrancer – for the remainder of the year kept busy as Senior Master of the Supreme Court, Queen's Bench Division – presides over the official scrutiny of the Coinage of the Realm.

In a ceremony dating back to at least 1280, and sadly not visible to the public, sample coins made the previous year at the Royal Mint are brought to Goldsmiths' Hall each February or March. They are then put into a box or pyx which is presented to a jury of goldsmiths. Each juryman, after being sworn in by the Remembrancer, is required to inspect the coins to ensure they are of the right size and the metal of an appropriate quality.

There is also good reason for suggesting that it was the Goldsmiths' seventeenth-century practice of using promissory notes in their dealings with each other which paved the way for modern financing. One of their number is regarded very much as the 'father of banking', the former Lord Mayor of London Sir Francis Child (1642–1713), who, inheriting a goldsmith's business founded as long ago as 1559, transformed it into a bank. While no longer independent, Child & Company opened for business 'at the Marygold by Temple Bar' in 1673, making it one of Europe's oldest banking houses.

HABERDASHERS' HALL

18 WEST SMITHFIELD, EC1

While every livery company still fortunate to have a hall has at some point decided to rebuild, or more commonly been forced to, only the Haberdashers have seen fit to do so in the twenty-first century. Another of the Great Twelve, the company was originally an offshoot of the greatest of them, the Mercers. Initially functioning as two separate but related divisions – as hurrers they made and sold hats while as milliners they imported fashionable apparel from Italy – the breakaway company was finally granted its own charter by Henry VI in 1448. By Elizabethan times it was also importing pins to replace thorns, and charging a sufficiently high price for them that gentlemen were forced to allow their ladies what became known as 'pin money' in order that they could pay for a regular supply.

The company's first hall was built a few years later, in 1461, and situated on the corner of Staining Lane and Maiden Lane (now Gresham Street). Like so many others it fell to the Great Fire, and once again its 1671 replacement was designed by Edward Jerman. Over the years this was extended and modified, particularly after it was again damaged by fire in 1840 and then 1864. The end came in 1940 with another fire following an air raid, after which a new hall, using panelling from the 1730s, was incorporated into an office development on the site.

Forty years later, by which time these offices were up for redevelopment, the decision was taken to acquire a new site in West Smithfield. Sir Michael Hopkins & Partners were commissioned to create a striking and imaginative new hall which was formally opened by the Queen in 2003.

Arranged around a properly secluded, cloistered courtyard (and in this regard like the same architect's Portcullis House at Westminster), the finished £7.7 million building is entirely contemporary yet in its layout and craftsmanship manages to reflect the long history of its occupants. Despite the apparent luxury of its spacious open courtyard, that same layout also illustrates pressures of working in such a confined space as the modern City: no fewer than six different party-wall agreements were necessary before work could start to shoehorn the new building in among the typically haphazard jumble of more conventional offices which already ringed the site.

That craftsmanship is evident everywhere one looks, not just in the 400,000 hand-made bricks with their traditional lime mortar, but also in the contours of its pitched roof which is clad in more than 700 diamond-shaped lead tiles. (With each of these almost 5ft from top to bottom and weighing in excess of 220lb, before anything was attempted on site a prototype roof section was erected as a try-out at Stanford-le-Hope in Essex.)

If one is lucky enough to gain entry, it is in the courtyard that you get the best possible vantage point from which to examine the finished roof. Its rich grey patina provides a striking contrast with the red walls – solid, and more than a foot thick – and with the green of the open space. Very much a triumph of old crafts and new technologies, behind the arched cloisters the interior too is a magnificent space with high vaulted oak ceilings, oak boards for floors and walls panelled in the same durable wood.

SKINNERS' HALL

8 DOWGATE HILL, EC4

Agreeing after a dispute to alternate with the rival Merchant Taylors for sixth and seventh places in the Great Twelve's order of precedence – hence, some say without much proof, the phrase 'at sixes and sevens' – the Skinners' Company received its first charter in 1327 since when it has sought control of the fur trade. The company's first hall on this site, burned down in 1666 in the Great Fire, was probably built in about 1380, this new façade on Dowgate Hill being applied by William Jupp to its replacement only in 1790. Beneath its Coade stone pediment, it is pleasing in its solidity, but from the pavement appears quite a modest building, particularly given the wealth which accrued to the company during those centuries when the use of fur, as an obvious indicator of the wearer's superiority and dignity, was restricted to the ruling classes.

In fact, and as can be seen round the corner in College Street, the Skinners' Hall goes back some distance from the street. The company's valuable property interests being these days still largely centred around this building and the neighbouring offices, the Skinners have retained a good portion of it for themselves so that one of the arches giving on to the hill provides access to not one but two courtyards in addition to the usual generously proportioned banqueting and reception rooms.

Of these the Banqueting Hall is the most impressive, housing a collection of monumental paintings by Sir Frank Brangwyn which tells the story of the company and fur from the earliest times. Far more elegant, however, is the so-called Outer Hall with its slender circular gallery arranged around a chandelier which was made in about 1780 in one of the glass factories supplying Catherine the Great. Originally a gift to the Ambassador to St Petersburg, Sir James Harris (1746–1820) – later the 1st Earl of Malmesbury – it was given to the company by the 5th Earl's heir, Viscount Fitzharris.

As for Dowgate Hill itself, the name provides the best clue as to why the Skinners would have been here in the first place. Being derived from the name of a dock or watergate close to where the Walbrook entered the Thames, this stream would have provided the necessary source of water for lowly workers known as 'tawyers' – definitely members of the labouring classes rather than of the company – to carry out the deeply unpleasant processes involved in cleaning the raw skins.

For similar reasons, the Dyers', Innholders' and Tallow Chandlers' Halls are nearby, although the Walbrook itself has long disappeared from view. No longer the 'fair brook of sweet water' which John Stow described in 1598, it is now known more prosaically as the London Bridge Sewer, this despite ordinances going back as far as 1288 requiring it to be made free of dung. Its course can still be determined on a map, however, by tracing the boundary of the Walbrook and Dowgate wards.

TO GOD ONLY BEALL GLORY

VINTNERS' HALL

UPPER THAMES STREET, EC4

Unfortunately located on one of the City's least pleasant roads, the Vintners' Hall has in one form or another been standing on this site for nearly 650 years – but one suspects that few of the thousands who drive past every day notice it. While the Vintners' Company was not to receive its royal charter until 1364 – a grant giving it a monopoly on trade with Gascony in wine, cloth and herrings – it already had a hall. The original had been built in 1357 on the site which nearly ninety years later was to be bequeathed to the company in the will of Guy Shuldham, citizen and vintner of London. Rebuilt following the Great Fire, the new hall was again substantially remodelled in 1822 when the widening of Upper Thames Street led to the loss of some rooms. The façade and entrance we see today, however, are newer still and date only from 1910.

Notwithstanding these later modifications, and some considerable work needed to deal with an infestation of deathwatch beetle, the Vintners' Court Room is still nevertheless one of the oldest rooms in the City. The greater part of its carvings date from the rebuilding after the Great Fire, and much of the furniture – including an elaborate cased clock, pier glasses and several coats of arms in the cornices – is early eighteenth century. To good effect an attempt was also made after the Second World War (when the hall was fortunate enough to escape serious damage) to replace the Victorian stained glass and to eliminate some of the more obvious nineteenth-century alterations.

The origins of the Vintners' Company are reasonably obscure, although it is known that it was originally in two parts, the *Vinterarii* (wine importers) and the *Tabernarii* (tavernkeepers). The former were to prove pre-eminent, perhaps unsurprisingly at a time when the wine trade was of such importance to the medieval economy that for a while in the 1440s it accounted for a full third of England's entire imports.

Inevitably over time this influence diminished. Edward VI curtailed the company's rights to sell wine; its support for Charles I meant it suffered under the Parliamentarians; and a further curtailment of privileges was enacted by Charles II and his brother James II. The company's financial standing was also badly damaged by the Great Fire, which destroyed not only the hall but many of its other properties.

Today, however, a certain pride in its former status is much in evidence and entirely understandable. Thus in the building itself is a large painting depicting a Mr Van Horn who successfully embodies the spirit of the company, having reportedly drunk 35,680 bottles of wine before dying at the age of ninety. Similarly, in memory of an occasion in the fourteenth century when the company is said to have feasted at one sitting the kings of England, Scotland, France, Denmark and Cyprus, its members traditionally cheer five times instead of three when drinking the loyal toast.

'The only things more cushioned than the venerable armchairs are the members'

Jeremy Paxman,
*Friends in High Places:
Who Runs Britain?*
1991

7
PRIVATE PLACES
Members Only

THE ATHENAEUM

107 PALL MALL, SW1

Once somewhat spitefully described as a place 'where all the arts and sciences are understood, except gastronomy', of all the traditional West End clubs the Athenaeum has never enjoyed a reputation for luxury, or for social prestige – it's far too serious for anything so frivolous – or even for offering its members any real opportunity to enjoy themselves. In fact, what it is best known for is its bishops, this despite having the most outstanding club library (both in terms of contents and ambience) in one of central London's architecturally most distinguished *palazzos* and on a matchless site overlooking Waterloo Place.

The *palazzo* in question – though not the rather clumsy attic which was added seventy years later – is by Decimus Burton, who also designed much of the furniture. It was completed in 1830 and with its most prominent feature a handsome porch of paired Doric columns surmounted by a gilded figure of Pallas Athene (inside there is another, of Apollo), it has long been regarded as one of Britain's best Classical Revival buildings.

As for the mitres, well even in the early 1960s members were protesting that there weren't that many of them – only thirty, they said, plus half a dozen archbishops – and, indeed, then as now bishops were easily outnumbered by boffins. Arguing against the numbers, however, is the experience of R.A. Butler who, repairing there for lunch after being appointed Churchill's Chancellor of the Exchequer in 1951, reported that he and two companions 'ate what remained of the Club food after the bishops had had their run; for we were somewhat late, and the bishops attack the sideboards early'.

Notwithstanding the comedy inherent in such a vision of voracious bishops swooping down on to the buffet, the club has always been considered rather stuffy. In a sense that is scarcely surprising, for its foundation in 1824 was expressly to provide somewhere 'for the association of individuals known for their scientific or literary attainments'. Accordingly, at least seven future prime ministers were among the early recruits, later joined by Dickens, Darwin and Trollope. (Famously, the latter was reluctantly persuaded to kill off the Bishop of Barchester's wife after hearing two of his fellow members – clergymen as it happens – discussing how boring they found her.) That said, the undeniably rakish Sir Richard Burton was a member of the Athenaeum too, the explorer and collector of pornography reportedly translating his *Arabian Nights* in the South Library. So too was J.M.W. Turner who was in the habit of downing an entire bottle of vintage port on his own. But in general its reputation seems secure as a place for the great and the good to foregather rather than the rakehells. Even Turner, after all, insisted the steward extinguish the candles in order that he could drink to excess without anyone watching him do it.

Sadly now lost to clubland is the Athenaeum's companion across the square, the equally splendid United Services Club whose Nash building has now devolved to the rather dull Institute of Directors. Until 1976, however, as the first military club in London, the 'Senior' was a natural watering-hole of choice for many Service upper echelons. Thus as Anthony Sampson recalls a member explaining: 'the last war was run by the Athenaeum on one side, with the scientists and civil servants, and the Senior on the other, with the admirals and generals. Since they all talked very loudly, it wasn't difficult to discover what was going on.'

THE BEEFSTEAK CLUB

9 IRVING STREET, WC2

In almost every regard, the architecturally modest Beefsteak is the Athenaeum's polar opposite. In place of Athene's grand temple to academic eminence, it has just a single dining table in a long, panelled, cream-coloured room above a shop. Similarly, while in areas of the Athenaeum conversation is frowned upon or even forbidden, at the Beefsteak it is the very point of the club. Finally, in Waterloo Place the overwhelming sense is one of imperial greatness, academic rigour and quiet self-importance, but the Beefsteak has its origins in the so-called 'thunder and lightning room' above the old Covent Garden Theatre.

There the dissimilarities end, however, for in terms of their intellectual achievements, social status and professional distinction, the members of the Beefsteak give nothing away to the Athenaeum or indeed to any other club. For a while, indeed, election to the Beefsteak was so exclusive – restricted to just two dozen members – that as Prince of Wales even the future George IV was obliged to bide his time until a vacancy occurred.

Founded by Hogarth and his friends in 1730, the original club failed after 137 years but was born again in 1876, since when it has rarely looked back. The membership is still only a few hundred, although with no bar at which to foregather (and only twenty able to sit down at a time) it is probable that many members have never actually met. In recent decades these have included the dukes of Beaufort and Devonshire, the Harolds Macmillan and Nicolson, and Sir Osbert Lancaster, as well as such literary giants as Kipling, Betjeman and Thomas Hardy, which might explain why, as the late Anthony Sampson was candid enough to admit, 'many of the junior members like me are too frightened actually to go there'.

Sadly, whether courageous or fearful, no member is any longer obliged to wear the club's picturesque uniform of blue coats and buff waistcoats (with buttons bearing the legend 'Beef & Liberty'). Many equally old traditions are maintained, however, including the habit of addressing all servants as 'Charles' to avoid confusion, and beefsteaks are naturally always on the menu.

For all that, the current building is no great shakes externally: an exercise in fake Jacobean, or what has been called 'theatreland Lycean'. Designed by Frank Verity, the son of a noted cinema designer, it is indeed by far the most modest of the leading clubs – with the possible exception of Pratt's. But while Pratt's (q.v.) is a basement dive, it at least has a respectable address in St James's. By contrast the Beefsteak is, to say the least, more than a little seedy: a modest doorway opening on to a nondescript pedestrian street running into central London's least smart square.

All of which lends credence to the most celebrated Beefsteak anecdote, namely that after observing a succession of old men entering premises opposite a strip joint and emerging a couple of hours later looking happy, relaxed and all's-well-with-the-world, the police decided to raid the place.

Once inside, it is said, they found four gentlemen sitting beneath the beams, and asked each of them for his particulars.

'I am the Lord Chancellor,' said the first of them.

'Yes, and you sir?'

'The Archbishop of Canterbury.'

'Oh yes, and the next?'

'I am the Governor of the Bank of England.'

'I see, and I suppose you are the Prime Minister?'

'In point of fact I am,' replied A.J. Balfour, before returning to No. 10.

It would be foolish to expect anyone to spoil such a splendid yarn, least of all when it is about his own club, and indeed the only single fact ever to have been disputed about this tale is that the archbishop of the day was never a member. But of course he could always have gone as a guest . . .

BOODLE'S

28 ST JAMES'S STREET, SW1

From the pavement perhaps the most elegant building in clubland, and this despite a modern, slightly jarring extension overlooking the Economist Building of 1964, Boodle's, along with White's and Brooks's, is one of only three survivors of the eighteenth-century coffeehouse culture which first gave birth to the gentleman's club. Designed by the otherwise little known John Crunden, its decidedly Adam-style clubhouse with its distinctive Venetian window dates from 1775–6. It was originally built for a celebrated gaming club with a reputation for high stakes, but the Savoir Vivre is thought to have failed as a result of an extended period of austerity on the run-up to Britain's defeat in the American Revolution (1776–83).

Boodle's hastily took its place, and having been evocatively described in Queen Victoria's day as 'a sweet old mahogany and wax candle kind of place' it has managed to retain much of the same feel and atmosphere. It takes its name from head waiter Edwin Boodle, a Shropshire publican's son who ran the original premises on behalf of its owner, the social entrepreneur William Macall. The early membership was largely drawn from one of Macall's other famous establishments, Almack's in Pall Mall, the Scotsman having changed his name about to conceal his unfashionable origins. With the subscription set at a hefty 3 guineas, a number of curious rules were in force. Strangers, for example, were welcome in the club only between 1 May and 1 November, with only one guest per member at a time and with each guest paying for himself.

In 1905 Baroness Orczy is said to have based her mysterious, heroic Scarlet Pimpernel, Sir Percy Blakeney, on a Boodle's member of her acquaintance. Half a century later the club very obviously provided the model for 'Blade's' in James Bond folklore, with 007's boss 'M' habitually coming here for 'his usual meagre luncheon – a grilled Dover sole followed by the ripest spoonful he could gouge from the club Stilton'. Bond's Old Etonian creator lunched here too, apparently more often than he did not. But – international, urbane, a bit of a spy himself and undeniably dashing – Ian Fleming was far from being a typical member and admitted that what he wanted when he joined was a dull club. (Hence his leaving White's, since he found that up the road at No. 38 'they gas too much'.)

Instead Boodle's has for a very long time enjoyed a reputation for being a place for country gents, bucolic baronets and those fabled knights of the shires. So much so that even members joke that were one to look into the smoking room tomorrow and call, 'Cab for Sir Hugh', half of those inside would look up and think it was for him. Certainly Sir Hugh and his ilk must feel at home here, since the interior sports some excellent pictures – including a Stubbs – nearly all of which are of Grand National winners, Arcadian landscapes and other typically country-house subjects.

Similarly while as at White's the club's historic betting books contain details of wagers about the sanity of George III, scandalous affairs and other aspects of high society tittle-tattle, there are numerous others concerning the distance, by road, between one rural outpost and another, and even bets about the price of hay.

BROOKS'S

ST JAMES'S STREET, SW1

Across the street and sufficiently self-assured not to have a street number (it is actually at No. 60), Brooks's takes the whole country-house idea one step further still. Designed by Henry Holland, and a Whig stronghold when White's was political and Tory, it was once memorably described as being 'like a duke's house – with the duke lying dead upstairs'.

The living dukes are meanwhile mostly downstairs, and there are quite a few of them too, if not quite as many as at the Turf Club which for years held the record with sixteen. Just as at Boodle's where one duke is said to have enjoyed sitting in the window on rainy days 'watching the damn'd people getting wet', here another – the 9th Duke of Devonshire (1868–1938) – used to enjoy sitting in the hall wielding a cane with which he used to hit any members he disliked. Incredibly, few of his fellow members objected to such boorish behaviour, and indeed 'such is snobbism,' recorded his grandson in the 1980s, 'that those who he saw fit not to strike became resentful as it had become the in thing to be struck by the Duke of Devonshire'.

These days the conduct is generally better and more restrained. It's true that backgammon is still very popular, particularly among those older members who came on board when the St James's Club merged with Brooks's in 1975. Money may change hands too, albeit with none of the recklessness of the eighteenth century, when sitting at whist, faro, quinze and hazard Brooks's members were frequently and famously made or ruined.

The most notable of these was the politician Charles James Fox who in the 1770s sat at Brooks's for a full twenty-two hours playing hazard. At one point £12,000 to the good, he finished with the dice £11,000 down – an extraordinary sum for the day – then went to the Commons where he made, unsurprisingly, a very poor speech before returning to Brooks's for dinner. Following this he went straight on to White's where he drank until dawn before entering Almack's. There he won £6,000 which he immediately took to Newmarket and lost the lot on a horse. Relief came in 1774 when his father, then his mother and then his elder brother died, between them leaving him property, positions and a very considerable fortune. However, the entire £154,000 was already spoken for by his creditors, and he was soon back in debt.

Today Fox's ghost lingers over the members at Brooks's. Not just in his likeness by Nollekens in the staircase hall beneath a lovely, light glass dome, but also in the Great Subscription Room. Architecturally very much the pride of the club, with its coved ceiling and Venetian window, this was painstakingly restored after a fire with the original colours being copied from old Rowlandson prints. It still contains the original gaming table at which Fox sat, which can be recognised by the slice cut out of it (so many members insist) to accommodate his generous girth.

THE GARRICK CLUB

15 GARRICK STREET, WC2

Like the Beefsteak somewhat outside the geographically precise area of clubland proper – which since its creation has never been anywhere but St James's – the Garrick is nevertheless one of the better-known clubs in town, as well as the only one to have asked for the street to be named after it. Besides the famous salmon and cucumber tie, the Garrick's celebrity probably depends on there being so many loose-tongued lawyers and journalists among its members, so that compared with other clubs it is frequently written about in newspaper gossip columns. By far the most embarrassing of such occasions was during the 1987 *Spycatcher* débâcle when counsel for the defence claimed to have gathered useful intelligence about the prosecution's tactics simply by listening to the Attorney-General, Lord Havers, discussing his plan of attack while standing at the club urinal.

Founded in 1831 as 'a society in which actors and men of education and refinement might meet on equal terms', the Garrick originally met at Probatt's Family Hotel before moving to what was then still called New King Street. That was in 1864, at which time it was said to be the haunt of 'nearly all the leading actors', and by 1958 Cary Grant and Ingrid Bergman were being invited to film scenes for *Indiscreet* within its portals.

These days, though, the Garrick is probably too grand and entry too pricey for most actors to consider, although once inside Frederick Marrable's handsome Italianate clubhouse its theatrical heritage is still much in evidence. As well as paintings by Johann Zoffany of David Garrick and C.F. Reinhold, and a library full of historic playbills and theatrical biographies, there is on the main staircase a bust of Sir Henry Irving – this despite the great Shakespearian having been blackballed when he first applied to join.

Historically the club's most notorious members were not actors at all, however, but writers, namely Dickens and Thackeray. These two titans of Victorian respectability famously had a stand-up row in the Coffee Room – the Garrick still has the very table – after which each refused to acknowledge the other for more than fifteen years. Fortunately, a reconciliation was eventually effected when they spontaneously shook hands in the hall of the Athenaeum, and just in time, for two weeks later Dickens found himself a mourner at Thackeray's own final curtain.

Even leaving aside such quarrels, however, the Garrick in its day was rarely a stranger to controversy. The exotically named Lord de Roos, for example, was kicked out for cheating at cards. Journalist John Foster (whom a fellow member described as a 'low scribbler without an atom of talent and totally unsuited to the society of gentlemen') came perilously close to it after publishing details of a private Garrick dinner in his newspaper. Best of all, a Mr Sola was forced to tender his resignation after being accused by a housemaid of stealing the soap.

Happily the Garrick's 1,300 members these days seem to prefer conversation to kleptomania, to the point where they asked for the club table – at which those eating alone could enjoy the company of other similarly reluctant solo diners – to be narrowed by 6 inches in order that they could better hear each other. A nice touch, and typically Garrick.

THE NAVAL AND MILITARY CLUB

4 ST JAMES'S SQUARE, SW1

Its nickname being derived from the conspicuous lettering on the stone pillars outside its former home on Piccadilly, at the close of the last century the 'In and Out' acquired the freehold of what is now London's oldest clubhouse. Indeed, with St James's Square the prototype of the grand West End square, and at its north-east corner No. 4 the only house with its courtyard and mews still intact, this deceptively large and precious architectural survivor dates from 1676.

After a fire in December 1725 (when the Prince of Wales rallied a detachment of footguards to fight the flames and beat off looters), the original building was remodelled for the Duke of Kent with a number of leading architects spoken of in connection with the work. The design itself, for example, is Edward Shepherd's (see Crewe House). But Giacomo Leoni has links with it too, having been employed by the Duke on his Wrest Park, Bedfordshire, estate, while Nicholas Hawksmoor produced drawings for the Duke, and Sir Edwin Lutyens is thought to be the author of the later landscaping of what is now the members' surprisingly ample private garden.

Likewise, when it came to fitting out the highly distinguished interior which lies behind the discreet five-bay façade, the Duke employed a number of renowned artists and sculptors. These included J.M. Rysbrack, who is represented by a full-scale figure of Inigo Jones on the main staircase, John Boson and Henry Scheemakers who created a stunning baroque chimneypiece for the inner hall. With its rich plasterwork and Corinthian balusters the staircase was described as 'noble' by the notoriously picky Horace Walpole after his visit in 1761. And today it looks even finer, with the insertion of an elegant screen of pillars connecting it to the inner hall.

The screen was one of several important changes introduced by the 2nd Earl de Grey who inherited the house in 1833. Its success was only to be expected perhaps as he was the founding president of the (now Royal) Institute of British Architects as well as a serving member on various committees overseeing Nash's rebuilding of the 'Senior' in 1827, Edward Blore's remodelling of Buckingham Palace twenty years later, and the rebuilding of the Houses of Parliament.

For all its many architectural associations, however, and a wartime role as the headquarters for General de Gaulle's Free French forces, a blue plaque on its chaste Palladian façade means that today the name most associated with the house is Nancy Astor's – and clubmen can surely be forgiven for smiling if they think about that one for a moment. Not merely because the home of a leading 1930s female rights campaigner is now a gentlemen's club. Not even because what was once notorious as the meeting place for the discredited band of Hitler-appeasers known as the Cliveden Set – and into which at least one top Nazi (Ribbentrop) was welcomed – is now owned and enjoyed by the very men who fought with honour in the war which followed. But also because in what was once a bastion of teetotalism – invited for the weekend by the Astors, the Mosleys reputedly brought along a jerrycan full of martinis – the In and Out now boasts no fewer than three different bars.

At the same time Lady Astor's lovely panelled bedroom has become a private dining room, while there is also now a swimming pool in the mews, London's oldest squash court on the fourth floor, a subterranean billiard room, en-suite bedrooms for the members, two gyms and even private underground parking. All part of the process by which, as an architectural critic from *Country Life* observed, the club, 'itself a venerable feature of the London scene, has unlocked the potential of one of London's most impressive Palladian town houses'.

THE ORIENTAL

STRATFORD PLACE, W1

These days a sometimes congested cul-de-sac running off noisy Oxford Street is not perhaps the best location for anyone seeking peace and tranquillity. Nonetheless the Oriental – which Thackeray insisted was not merely the dullest club in London but actually proud to be so – has occupied Stratford House since 1962 and its members seem happy enough with the move. It must help that their previous home in Hanover Square was architecturally such a duffer that cabbies nicknamed it the Orizontal and that, unlike the Pall Mall clubs, the members own the freehold. Also that Stratford House – previously known as Aldborough House, then St Albans House and eventually Derby House, reflecting several distinguished previous owners – is large, luxurious and beautifully appointed with its Adam chimneypieces and some exceptional painted ceilings by Angelica Kauffmann.

It is also self-consciously grand, being in the words of Charles Graves who knew them all well 'as fine in quality as White's, Boodle's or Brooks's but with the space of infinitely larger clubs'. Thus in addition to having many generous, beautifully decorated rooms for entertaining, where once stood the last private ballroom to be built in London, it now has two whole floors of bedrooms. Just the job for members who aren't quite up to the journey home, like Ibrahim Pasha, perhaps, the son of Mehmet Ali Pasha, Viceroy of Egypt from 1804 to 1848. He was treated to dinner at the Oriental but, as one member put it, 'departed from the strict rules of the Prophet and became so elated that he had to be carried to the drawing room after dinner on the members' shoulders'.

In the 1840s, as this anecdote suggests, the club had firmer oriental connections than it has today, having been established in 1824 to give returning officers of the Honourable East India Company somewhere to socialise. Wishing to 'maintain that respectability and those comforts which their station in Society renders so essential', these chaps needed a club of their own because their military ranks were held 'in the East Indies only'. This meant that once back home they were ineligible for election to the Guards or United Services while the East India Club, now opposite the Naval and Military at 16 St James's Square, was not due to open its doors for another quarter of a century.

In any event, after it had opened the East India insisted on maintaining its martial character and was soon to boast no fewer than a dozen members with the Victoria Cross. By contrast the Oriental expanded to admit businessmen or 'boxwallahs' as members, as well as soldiers, particularly once the Honourable East India Company had been wound up after the Mutiny of 1857. A couple of years later three hedgehogs also became honorary members whom the committee 'obtained for the kitchen, to kill the black beetles'.

PRATT'S

14 PARK PLACE, SW1

'So you belong to Pratt's, do you?' asked journalist Duncan Fallowell. 'No, it belongs to me. The 10th Duke bought it in 1937.' So ran a memorable exchange with the late Duke of Devonshire in which, with characteristic wit and charm, Andrew Robert Buxton Cavendish staked his claim to London's most inviting basement. Comprising just a single, cluttered but decidedly cosy and cheerful club room, with an old-fashioned kitchen range off to one side and a modest, candle-lit dining room off to the other, the club behind the anonymous black front door traces its origins back to 1841. The occasion was when the 7th Duke of Beaufort, 'being bored with his usual haunts' – he was a founder member of the Garrick – took some friends and called at the home of his sometime steward, William Nathaniel Pratt. The Duke and his friends tarried, sitting in Pratt's kitchen and whiling away the hours in conversation and gaming.

Thus was set a pattern which, more or less uninterrupted, has continued there ever since. Even now the basement opens only in the evening, and in the spirit of the Duke, who was in no hurry to move on, it closes only once the last member has wandered out into the street above to see the sun rise. And while on the floors above there is now a comfortably appointed committee room and a billiard room, the former is used only very rarely, while the latter is mostly just somewhere for members to leave their coats and bags. Instead, the focus at Pratt's is now where it has always been, which is to say below street-level amid a beguiling jumble of old china, stuffed fish, antlers and antique prints.

As at the Beefsteak the servants share a single name to avoid confusion – this time each answers to the name George – and with just one table at which to dine members are seated as they arrive, thereby encouraging conversation among members who might not otherwise find themselves thrown together.

Pratt eventually died in 1860, leaving the running of the place to his widow and then his son, but in 1907 it was bought by one of its members, William Walsh. He carefully renovated the 'curious little club . . . with due regard for the old associations' before becoming the 4th Lord Ormathwaite and settling down to enjoy it. Thereafter he is said to have eaten here every night for nearly thirty years, recognising each of his several hundred members and insisting everyone – even the newest, youngest recruit – call him 'Willie'. After his death ownership passed to the Cavendishes who continue to cherish this uniquely relaxed and informal institution.

Its small size (only fourteen can dine at a time), along with a subscription which is still modest by St James's standards, mean the waiting list for Pratt's has traditionally been one of the longest in London. The joke being of course that what one gets at the end of the long wait is access to a basement and a very limited menu. There seems little doubt the quality of the company more than makes up for it, though. Cribbage is the only game allowed at this club which is traditionally favoured by smarter Tories and members of the Brigade of Guards, and the conversation is said rarely to reach the intellectual heights encountered at the Beefsteak. But nobody seems to mind, and the continuing popularity of Pratt's is not hard to discern.

THE REFORM CLUB

104 PALL MALL, SW1

By far the showiest club architecturally, but like the RAC and the Oxford and Cambridge far less intimate than the best of them, the Reform takes its name from the Bill of 1832 but owes its celebrity to Sir Charles Barry, *Penthouse* magazine and Jules Verne's Phileas Fogg. After winning a keenly fought competition it was the first of these who designed the clubhouse which opened in 1841. Just over thirty years later the last-named set off from here to voyage around the world in less than eighty days, and, a century later, the famous men's magazine was somehow able to photograph a nude on the staircase.

Barry based his design on the Farnese Palace in Rome, his preference being to arrange the principal rooms around a large open courtyard. Mindful of the English weather, however, he was eventually persuaded to glass this in – the eventual cost of the building was £80,000 against an estimate of less than £20,000 – so that today the club's main feature is this grand *cortile*. Rising through the building's full three-storey height it is certainly impressive: lofty but with its warm browns and yellows less forbidding than one might imagine. Around it are arranged cloisters giving on to the club's generously proportioned apartments, including a tripartite coffee room and a library, the finest room in the building. A wide gallery above the cloisters provides somewhere for members to gather to drink coffee and port in the afternoons.

Presenting a plain, solid face to the street but with a good measure of pomp and scale within, the Reform epitomises the staid values of the Victorian era and its clubs. In 1841, however, Barry's building was truly revolutionary, as radical in its own way as the Bill it celebrated. Creating an entirely new architectural vocabulary for the English urban landscape, Barry gave nineteenth-century London its first major *palazzo* elevation and in so doing quickly established a whole new set of rules for its builders.

As a result the six architects who lost out to Barry in the competition to design the Reform had not long to wait for something similar to come along. Thus by 1845 Sydney Smirke was working on the original Carlton Club next door, having with George Basevi already designed the rather more pompous Conservative Club around the corner at 74 St James's Street. Indeed Barry's lessons even crossed the border, James and David Hamilton producing for the Western Club in Glasgow a neat variation on a theme rising to an additional half-storey.

None, however, proved as successful as the original, nor as clever as the Reform in the way it blended classical architectural theories with the latest technologies. Thus Barry's clients enjoyed food prepared in advanced, mechanised kitchens designed by Alexis Soyer – in every sense England's first 'celebrity chef' – in which water was drawn, dishes warmed and even spits turned by steam. Meanwhile, out on the street, great flaming torches advertised the fact that Pall Mall was among the first of London's streets to have a mains gas supply. For an institution established to espouse the energy, drive and vibrancy of a new political and business elite – a grand club but never an exclusive one – it is hard to think of a more persuasive combination.

THE TRAVELLERS' CLUB
106 PALL MALL, SW1

Strictly speaking, election to membership of the Travellers' still requires candidates to have journeyed 500 miles in a straight line from London, a pretty stiff requirement at the time of its foundation but in our own (as Jeremy Paxman once observed) one 'fulfilled by any Ibiza package holidaymaker'. Nonetheless the Travellers' is an appealing place, and is unique among these otherwise private palaces in that it admits strangers if they telephone and book a tour. That said, many who visit will already be familiar with the finest room in the club because, with its Greek-style frieze and Roman columns, the club's elegant library – in what must be a major irritation for its members – has become a popular choice among television and film location hunters seeking unspoilt period interiors.

Another of Sir Charles Barry's designs, this time based on the Palazzo Pandolfini in Florence, the Travellers' actually pre-dates the Reform by a decade. Its plan, like the later building, is that of a *cortile* with the façade of an Italian Renaissance *palazzo*, but it is built on a more modest scale and with a stucco finish in place of its neighbour's smooth and costlier Portland ashlar. Together with the Athenaeum on its other side, however, the three make a collection of neo-Classical buildings whose style and quality are unmatched anywhere in the capital.

Founded in 1819, almost certainly at the suggestion of Foreign Secretary Lord Castlereagh, the intention was to create 'a point of reunion for gentlemen who have travelled abroad and to afford them the opportunity of inviting as honorary visitors the principal members of all foreign missions and travellers of distinction'. The defeat of Napoleon Bonaparte had made such things possible, although the members were initially forced to share 'a shabby low-roomed house' at No. 49.

Following the completion in 1832 of Barry's splendid clubhouse, however, the distinguished visitors began to arrive and a handrail attached to the balustrade of the main staircase recalls the most famous of them, the octogenarian French Ambassador Prince Talleyrand-Perigord, who spent a good deal of time here in the early 1830s playing whist with friends.

Heads of foreign missions in London are still invited to take temporary advantage of the club's hospitality while accredited to the Court of St James, and Britain's own diplomats and Foreign Office officials are also well represented among the membership. Lord Lytton and Thackeray, however, were blackballed – a hostile member declaring, 'we don't want any writing fellows here' – along with the painter Landseer, Sir Cecil Rhodes and Lord Randolph Churchill.

Finally, while many a man looks upon his club as a sort of home from home, it's worth noting that in recent times only the Travellers' has proved sufficiently welcoming actually to fulfill that role. The cosmopolitan cleric, armorist and keen huntsman Monsignor Alfred Gilbey lived here full time until his death in 1998, even being allowed by the committee to construct his own private chapel in a former boot-room with Cardinal Heenan giving him special licence to receive the Blessed Sacrament. In return the 96-year-old always claimed he was happier at the Travellers' than at his other clubs – the Athenaeum, and Buck's in Mayfair – both of which he thought were above him: the one intellectually and the other socially.

WHITE'S

37–8 ST JAMES'S STREET, SW1

Older than the Bank of England and the Union with Scotland, and after more than 300 years still, as its biographer Percy Colson described it, 'an oasis of civilisation in a desert of democracy', White's is the pre-eminent London club and has been since its foundation in 1693. Originally a chocolate rather than a coffee house, it was run by Italian Francesco Bianco or Francis White who charged twopence for entry when a penny was the norm. Thereafter with private members quickly ousting the public it rapidly became exclusive, albeit as a place where, as Edward Harley, 2nd Earl of Oxford put it, 'young noblemen were fleeced and corrupted by fashionable gamblers and profligates'.

Certainly high play was important from the earliest days and, while the stakes were rarely as stratospheric or the conduct quite as reckless as at Brooks's, its eighteenth-century betting books tell a tale or two. The Duke of Portland, for example, won a phenomenal £200,000 at one sitting, keeping a clear head for his cards by drinking only water. By contrast George Harley Drummond, on the first and only occasion he played at the club, was forced to resign from the family bank after losing to Beau Brummel a comparatively modest £20,000, while in the 1750s Sir John Bland of Kippax Park in Yorkshire died by his own hand when his gambling debts were threatening the future of his extensive estates.

Initially the club spent a few peripatic years at various different addresses in St James's Street until, arriving on its present site in 1755, it ordered the structure to be rebuilt to the designs of James Wyatt in 1787. Remodelled again in 1811, when the front door was moved down the hill and its place taken by the famous bow window, the façade was reworked once more in 1852, this time by James Lockyer with sculptural decorations provided by Sir George Scharf. Inside it is small but beguiling, with a beautiful understated coffee room and an exceptionally elegant eighteenth-century staircase. Also some nice touches, such as the oldest billiard table in the world, and in each room the sort of patina and smart yet congenial atmosphere other clubs can only hope to acquire over the coming centuries.

George IV, William IV and Edward VII were all members, so too was every prime minister in all thirty-two administrations from Walpole to Peel. More recently Prince Charles had his stag night here. Little wonder then that the club has a certain relaxed arrogance – for example, refusing an earlier Prince of Wales permission to smoke in the morning room – and on occasion this attitude has cost the members dear.

In 1869 the Prince merely went off in a huff to form the rival Marlborough Club, but two years later when Henry William Eaton was blackballed he took far more drastic action. Rumoured to have driven an omnibus before making his fortune, after being ennobled as Baron Cheylesmore he retaliated by buying the freehold for £46,000 – the members had offered only £38,000 – and putting up the rent. The error quickly recognised, hasty approaches were made to admit his son but Henry turned them down and raised the rent again. The same offer was made to the 3rd Lord Cheylesmore, an Old Etonian and a major-general in the Brigade of Guards. He accepted but then, in deference to his father, refused to take up his membership and raised the rent once more. In fact not until 1927 were the members finally able to buy their clubhouse, and even then only because the 4th Lord Cheylesmore was leaving England behind and removing to Canada.

'**In London it was necessary to construct all kinds of strongholds under or above ground** '

Sir Winston Churchill,
Their Finest Hour,
1949

8
IMPERIAL ERECTIONS
Bring on the Military Men

THE CHARTERHOUSE

CHARTERHOUSE SQUARE, EC1

Having survived both the Great Fire and the Blitz of 1940–1, this small religious relic clinging to the edge of the City is now the only monastic estate in London to survive in anything like its original medieval form. That said, for the last 400 years it has been a retirement home, and in one sense is a pseudo-military establishment being for those delightfully described as 'decrepit Captaynes either at Sea or Land, and Souldiers maymed or ympotent'.

Originally it was a Carthusian monastery, founded in 1371 by Sir Walter de Manny. Following the Protestant Reformation, during which one monk was forcibly starved to death and its last prior became the first of 105 Catholic martyrs to be executed at Tyburn, it passed through a number of aristocratic hands. Then in 1611 it was bought by Thomas Sutton, a City merchant originally from Knaith in Lincolnshire. 'Esteemed the richest commoner in England', he paid £13,000 for the property and in his will provided it with an endowment to create a school for forty-four poor boys and an almshouse for impoverished gentlemen. In 1872 the school, still known as Charterhouse, relocated to Godalming in Surrey, and three years later the buildings were taken over by another, the Merchant Taylors' School, until it too left London.

Forty pensioners still remain, however, at what is also called Sutton's Hospital (or the Hospital of King James), including until his death in 2001 the novelist Simon Raven. They are correctly called Brothers, each having a cell overlooking the main courtyard and the promise of 'a full library and a full stomach, and the peace and quiet in which to enjoy them both'. Visitors are welcome to join them on one or two guided tours held each Wednesday during the summer months, but for the rest of the year the Brothers enjoy the sort of peace and seclusion only an Oxbridge college could provide (and even then only when free of tourists, and of course of undergraduates).

With their ancient gardens the buildings are well worth a visit. Queen Elizabeth I really did sleep here, in 1561, as a guest of Sir Edward North who was ruined by the expense and had to sell up and retire to the country. James I also stayed here and, after being proclaimed king in the Great Chamber, created 133 new knights on the spot. Situated above the seventeenth-century library, this Great Chamber is said to have been the best Elizabethan interior in the country before it was bombed in 1941.

More than anything, though, the complex of old school and monastic outbuildings presents a welcome contrast to the noise of the City and to the bold Victorian baroque of nearby Smithfield. Part of the west wall of the Carthusian cloister remains, including three entrances to what would have been monks' dwellings as Carthusians have separate, small houses with their own private gardens; also the sixteenth-century Wash House Court and the original priory gatehouse. This, with its strong oak door, is actually fifteenth century but with upper storeys added in the eighteenth when, with pleasing economy, this portion was again recycled by being absorbed into a domestic dwelling. Now, inevitably, it has been reborn again as offices.

THE CITADEL

HORSE GUARDS PARADE, SW1

Right there on the Mall and so conspicuous that, paradoxically, few people actually notice it, the distinctive ivy-clad Citadel at the far end from Buckingham Palace nevertheless remains one of central London's most enigmatic and unknown buildings. Constructed for the Admiralty in 1940–1, and designed in consultation with W.A. Forsyth, beneath the greenery it is built of compressed pebble and flint blocks, and as something of an architectural iceberg extends at least as far underground as it does on top.

Intended above all to provide protection against attack for the Admiralty's confidential communications systems, it was in the opinion of writer and Naval Intelligence expert Donald McLachlan 'probably the best bomb-proof headquarters in London. [With] officers and civilians and "secret ladies" cut off by twenty feet of steel and concrete from the fresh air of St James's Park [but with] the assurance of safety from even a direct hit – and a bracing assurance it was.'

However, a claustrophic environment was the price they paid for that assurance, the Citadel with its absence of windows, daylight or any sound of traffic or of life outside forming an important part of the response to Churchill's call for a network of 'bomb-proof strongholds capable of housing the whole essential staffs of many departments of state'.

The construction of these he entrusted to his old friend Lord Beaverbrook, though he was later to admit that many were not completed until long after the air raids were over, and that very few were used during the V1 and V2 attacks of 1944 and 1945. He recognised their value in terms of propaganda and morale-building, however, declaring in 1949 'it was good to feel we had them under our lee'. Altogether, under Beaverbrook's watch, a dozen of these strongholds were completed, several of them connected by tunnels, joining three others which had been built in the suburbs in 1933. (One, at Dollis Hill, was still in use half a century later when Britain went to war with Argentina.) Similarly it was on the advice of another of the old man's favourites, his comrade-in-arms Josiah Wedgwood V, that Parliament was persuaded of the need for what became the Cabinet War Rooms.

The design and fabrication of the Citadel were left to the tenants and were accordingly undertaken by the Admiralty itself. Perhaps this explains its use of slightly novel materials and why Churchill – who as previously observed was generally a great enthusiast for anything underground – felt able to be a little rude about its appearance when it came to writing his war memoirs. In fact what he called it was 'the vast monstrosity which weighs upon the Horse Guards Parade', wryly observing 'the demolition of whose twenty-foot-thick steel and concrete walls will be a problem for future generations when we reach a safe world'.

In the event of course the problem was put off, and for even longer than Churchill might have imagined. As a result, and in much the same way that the Home Counties are still scarred by the gaunt husks of disused pillboxes – ugly, frequently in the way but now regarded with something approaching nostalgia – the relative indestructibility of the Citadel has enabled this extraordinary if quite unlovely building to survive long beyond the war which gave it meaning.

MI6 BUILDING

85 VAUXHALL CROSS, SE1

It seems the members of Britain's Secret Intelligence Service have either finally perfected the art of concealment or the whole thing is nothing more than an expensively elaborate blind: Babylon-on-Thames (Terry Farrell's now world-famous MI6 building – more correctly, 85 Vauxhall Cross) is blatantly obvious yet apparently secure and highly secretive.

Indeed, the place has never been better described than by London's most inventive biographer, Iain Sinclair, identifying the 1995 design as 'an Inca jukebox . . . a hybrid of Gotham City and Alhambra fascist chic'. His own conclusion about the building is also strangely tempting, namely that the building is a fake, a front, and that the real work of the Secret Services, what he calls 'the wet jobs and the black propaganda', goes on somewhere else altogether: 'above a betting-shop in Stepney, a suite of unlet offices in Holborn'. Certainly, even during the rush hours you only very rarely see anyone entering or leaving the place; too few one would have thought to support the official claim that as many as 2,300 people work in this highly idiosyncratic, green and honey-coloured postmodernist ziggurat.

Against that, however, is the experience of London cabbies who claim to be dropping people off here on a regular basis, although when pressed more than a few have observed that when people want to get here they never actually ask for it by name or number but instead ask for the building next door or the bus stop round the corner on Vauxhall Bridge. Its postal address is similarly vague: PO Box 1300, London SE1 1BD.

Even so, for the rest of us, it is hard to believe that in 1995 government spooks would willingly have moved into a building which screams 'look at me' across the river. Or for that matter that they could have agreed to their new home – which apparently they call 'Legoland' – being featured in not one but two James Bond films. Instead, say conspiracy theorists, the building is just one big, £200 million joke at the public's expense.

Nonetheless, events have shown that whatever goes on in Sir Terry's building he must have designed it with attack in mind, for the structure is something of an authentic modern-day fortress. As many as five floors run below street level to provide maximum protection for the inhabitants and their equipment. Above ground it features bomb- and bullet-proof walls and windows and, it is said, some kind of wire mesh sandwich to prevent electromagnetic information from passing in or out. These defences have been put to the test too, specifically on the evening of 20 September 2000 when 85 Vauxhall Cross came under attack from a Russian-built rocket-propelled grenade launcher on its landward side, fired by the Real IRA. It hit the building on the eighth floor, but the only damage was to one small window.

POLICE STATION LANTERN

TRAFALGAR SQUARE, SW1

Even now only senior members of the royal family and the King's Troop Royal Horse Artillery are permitted to pass through Marble Arch. This means no policemen can, thus giving the lie to the commonly held belief that the interior of John Nash's arch used to house a tiny police station in its upper section. In fact, the smallest police station in the capital is here, in London's most famous open space, housed in a decorative, granite-clad lamp-post in the south-east corner of Trafalgar Square. Indeed, with room inside for just one and equipped with a direct line to Cannon Row, this strange little structure once genuinely laid claim to be the smallest police station in the world.

Installed here as a Metropolitan Police lookout post, it was intended to help the authorities keep an eye on the many marches and demonstrations which terminated in the square. (This tradition continued in spite of Sir Charles Barry's massive fountains which had been designed to deny potentially riotous assemblies the necessary room to gather.)

Sadly neither the large polygonal lantern on the top nor its companions at each corner of the square are as is popularly supposed from Nelson's flagship, *Victory*. If one peers through the windows at the cramped interior it seems that the police station has been ceded to the square's cleaners for them to use it as a store. Besides the curious fact of its existence, there isn't much to see of the station once you find it. Instead visitors are better off taking the opportunity to wander around Trafalgar Square, a space whose utter familiarity means that even first-time visitors tend to take it for granted thereby missing many of its small peculiarities.

The statue of Charles I, for example, is the square's oldest and, modelled on one of Henry IV on the Pont Neuf, was carved by Le Sueur in 1633. Rescued by Charles II after being hidden during the Civil War, it occupies the site of the original Eleanor or Charing Cross, a plaque on the ground marking it as the very point from which all distances from London are measured. Nearby is Major-General Sir Henry Havelock (1795–1857), who during the Indian Mutiny of 1857 marched an incredible 120 miles in nine days to relieve Cawnpore and then Lucknow before dying the following morning. Regarded by many as London's finest outdoor statue, his is also the first of its kind to be copied from a photograph.

Finally, the Nelson Column itself. At 145ft (plus another 17ft for the Admiral) it is still the tallest Corinthian column in the world. Carved in granite from Foggin Tor in Devon, most visitors know the reliefs at its base are cast from cannon captured during his many battles. But how many, one wonders, know who carved his likeness? The most famous statue in Britain? E.H. Baily surely deserves to be a household name.

ROYAL ARTILLERY
BARRACKS
GRAND DEPOT ROAD, SE18

Suggested as a possible venue for the shooting events in the 2012 Olympics, London's widest residential building is also among its least known, and this despite Nikolaus Pevsner himself having agreed that the scale 'can be compared only to St Petersburg'. In fact the design of this record-breaking and reassuringly forceful Classical façade of brick and colonnades – while an incredible 1,060ft in length, and able to accommodate nearly 4,000 officers and men and 1,718 horses – is quite simple, comprising a series of six modular sections spread out either side of a central, triumphal arch. Of thirteen, twenty-one and thirteen bays respectively, each block of three is connected by low white colonnades.

Commissioned by Lieutenant Colonel Conway of the Ordnance Department in 1774, and with later work supervised by the Duke of Richmond as his Master General, the whole building was devised in response to an urgent need to accommodate a corps of more than 3,200 which by 1716 were to be found in and around the Royal Arsenal and Royal Military Academy.

Originally just three of the six modules were completed, and this in the early 1780s when soldiers were camped in St James's Park for fear of anti-Catholic rioting. The remaining three were not constructed until some time later, probably in about 1802, the assumption being that this was done under the watch of James Wyatt who, as the first professional to be involved here in a permanent, official capacity, was appointed Architect to the Ordnance.

The central arch originally gave on to the ancillary buildings which, now mostly gone, were organised to the rear in order to maintain the classic purity and smart, military appearance of the façade. It was almost the size of a small town: wash- and cookhouses, stabling and several riding schools, magazines, workshops and a hospital would have been laid out on a grid pattern not unlike a Roman fort. The arch itself, however, is not impressive. Too short to dominate a frontage of this height and length, a little feeble in its execution, it also lacks the Palladian delicacy of William Kent's Horse Guards or the depth and richness of detail of, for example, the later Archway Block at Stonehouse Marines Barracks in Plymouth by Colonel G. Greene.

Nevertheless in its day the biggest building of its kind in the realm and one of the largest in the whole of Europe, the scale and grandeur of the Barracks are such that they seem quite un-English. Together with the immense parade ground, and all of it so close to potential popular or political opposition in London, anywhere else in Europe such a structure might in its day have suggested the threat of independent militarism. In the England of the eighteenth and nineteenth centuries, however, there appear to have been few such worries, perhaps because (engaged as it was in peacetime in its constitutionally correct role as overseer of the country's coastal defences) the Royal Regiment of Artillery had no interest in involving itself in issues of civil unrest. As a result, what might have been perceived as one of the most bombastic offsprings of the military-industrial complex is instead now seen as one of the more impressive survivors of Britain's imperial age.

ST JOHN'S GATE

ST JOHN'S LANE, EC1

ike a small castle defending the northern borders of the City, what since 1831 has been the headquarters of the Order of St John was formerly the south or main gatehouse for the great Priory of Clerkenwell. Indeed, it was to this very spot that the Patriarch of Jerusalem, Heraclius, came in 1185 to consecrate a round church which stood nearby and to ask Henry II for military assistance in protecting his city against Saladin.

Founded at about this time by a French knight, Jordan de Briset, of the original priory only the late Gothic gatehouse, a small part of the chancel and the Norman crypt now survive. The first of these was built in 1504 by Grand Prior Sir Thomas Docwra, but sadly very little of what we now see is actually his structure. Instead it has been much restored so that the Tudor-style interiors, for instance, are Victorian recreations by John Oldrid Scott.

Most of its history since the Dissolution has indeed been somewhat unhappy, a fact perhaps prefigured by the death of its prior William Weston on the very day that the act closing his order in England passed through Parliament. In July 1845 there were calls for the entire building to be pulled down since, under the terms of another new act, it had been declared a dangerous structure. Worse still, when a notice was circulated that unless it was put into substantial repair it would be demolished, a public subscription directed towards this purpose raised a wholly inadequate sum.

Nor, 250 years earlier, had the building been accorded any more respect. For example, for more than thirty years it was used as offices by Edward Tylney, Master of the Revels to Elizabeth I, who held rehearsals in the Great Hall. Later Hogarth's father ran a coffee house in a room above the gateway and from 1731 to 1781 it housed a printing works producing Edward Cave's *Gentleman's Magazine*. At that time employed in an upper room, Samuel Johnson, reportedly too shabby to be seen, ate and worked behind a screen. In the same room his pupil from Lichfield, David Garrick, gave his first performance in London – to a group of workmen. Finally, in the nineteenth century part of it was given over to a tavern, appropriately called The Jerusalem.

Since 1877 it has followed a more noble calling, however, as the home of the St John Ambulance Association, an offshoot of the original military Order. Here visitors can see the chapel containing the figure from Prior Weston's tomb, a library of early books and manuscripts off the original (1504) spiral staircase, as well as a museum. Exploring more than 900 years of the Knights Hospitallers' military, medical and religious histories, the most significant exhibits include a bronze cannon given to the Order by Henry VIII (presumably in happier times), knights' armour worn from the defence of Rhodes and Malta, and the beautifully illuminated charter depicting Philip II and Mary Tudor restoring the Order in 1557. There are also surviving fragments of the original medieval stonework, along with wood carvings, tiles and stained glass.

WELLINGTON ARCH

HYDE PARK CORNER, SW1

At different times called Wellington, Constitution and even Green Park Arch – and occasionally mistaken for Marble Arch at the other end of Park Lane – Decimus Burton's 1828 design was originally installed by Apsley House before increasing traffic levels caused it to be moved to its present position at the top of Constitution Hill in 1883. Intended as an act of homage to the Iron Duke, when completed it was crowned by a colossal bronze by M.C. Wyatt and his son showing the old soldier on the field at Waterloo and seated on his favourite horse, Copenhagen. Three years in the making, weighing 40 tons and more than 30ft in height, it was so ugly that a Frenchman on seeing it reportedly declared, 'We have been avenged'. Clearly many others agreed as well, for in 1883 it was removed to Round Hill in Surrey where it was presented by the Prince of Wales to the Aldershot Division.

Its replacement was another, much smaller, bronze of man and horse by J.E. Boehm, one which can still be seen on the island site in the company of a bronze Guardsman, a Fusilier, a Dragoon and a Royal Highlander. As for the arch itself, it was eventually surmounted by another gigantic piece, in this case the Quadriga by Adrian Jones, which is widely regarded as one of the most successful and elegant groups of its sort in the country.

The cost of this was met by Lord Michelham, a Jewish banker who presented it in 1912 in memory of his friend Edward VII. Indeed, it was his eleven-year-old son who provided the model for the figure, a winged representation of Peace pulling at the reins of the four spirited horses, inside one of which the sculptor famously hosted a dinner for eight upon the completion of his masterwork.

For many years, until the late 1990s when the structure was restored by English Heritage which opened it to the public, the top of the arch contained a small police station. Though considerably larger than the one in Trafalgar Square (q.v.), space was obviously still at a premium but was apparently sufficient for six police officers per shift with two so-called 'archers' on night duty. With occasional ceremonial duties, the six were chiefly called upon to keep the traffic moving round one of London's busiest road interchanges.

WOOLWICH GARRISON
WOOLWICH COMMON, SE18

Traditionally known as 'The Shop' to many generations of Army alumni, what was once the old Royal Military Academy traces its origins to a school for artillery officers which was established at Woolwich in 1719. Despite the Board of Ordnance's lofty-sounding aim and name – to institute, endow and support an academy, to be known as the Company of Gentlemen Cadets – it was housed in an old workshop of the Woolwich Warren and lacked a building of its own until a new barracks was built away from the river in 1752. The present building, however, dates only to 1805–8 and is the work of James Wyatt who as we have seen was very active in the area at this time. Once his work was completed the cadets received their training here for commissions in the Royal Artillery, later being joined by cadets destined for the Royal Engineers and the Royal Signals.

With a symmetrical north front originally 720ft in length, the building in yellow stock bricks comprises a central block connected by matching single-storey arcades to a pair of side blocks of nine bays. The two end pavilions, in red brick with stone details, are much later. Unsurprisingly, given its sheer size, it makes a grand and impressive sight. But perhaps because the central block with its four corner turrets and cupolas appears as a scaled-down caricature of the White Tower at the Tower of London, the entire assembly has been described as presenting 'a silly contrast to the Classicism of the Royal Artillery Barracks'.

An alternative view would be that, but for a hideous central clock, such a piece of Gothic whimsey is to be welcomed in such a military environment, and indeed from the earliest days the Academy found itself a stop on the tourist trail around the environs of London. Respected guidebooks, such as Mogg's *New Picture of London and Visitor's Guide to its Sights* (1844) described 'the sons of military men, and the more respectable classes, who are here instructed in mathematics, land-surveying, with mapping, fortification, engineering, the use of the musket and sword exercise, and field-pieces; and for whose use twelve brass cannon, three-pounders, are placed in front of the building, practising with which they acquire a knowledge of their application in the field of battle. This department is under the direction of a lieutenant-general, an instructor, a professor of mathematics, and a professor of fortification; in addition to which there are French, German, and drawing masters.'

It was then a mammoth establishment, although even as long ago as Mogg's day the prospect was being discussed of amalgamation with the Royal Military College at Sandhurst. In the event this did not take place for more than a hundred years, the merger finally being effected in 1947 after both establishments had reopened after the Second World War.

Today, however, its future uncertain, the old place at least lives on in the language. The phrase 'talking shop' derives from the academy's original nickname. Similarly snooker takes its name from mess slang for junior officers – *les neux* or the new boys – the rules having been devised by Field Marshal Sir Neville Chamberlain (1820–1902). He was an alumnus of the RMA, as indeed, slightly bizarrely, was the Prince Imperial, only son of Napoleon III and Empress Eugénie.

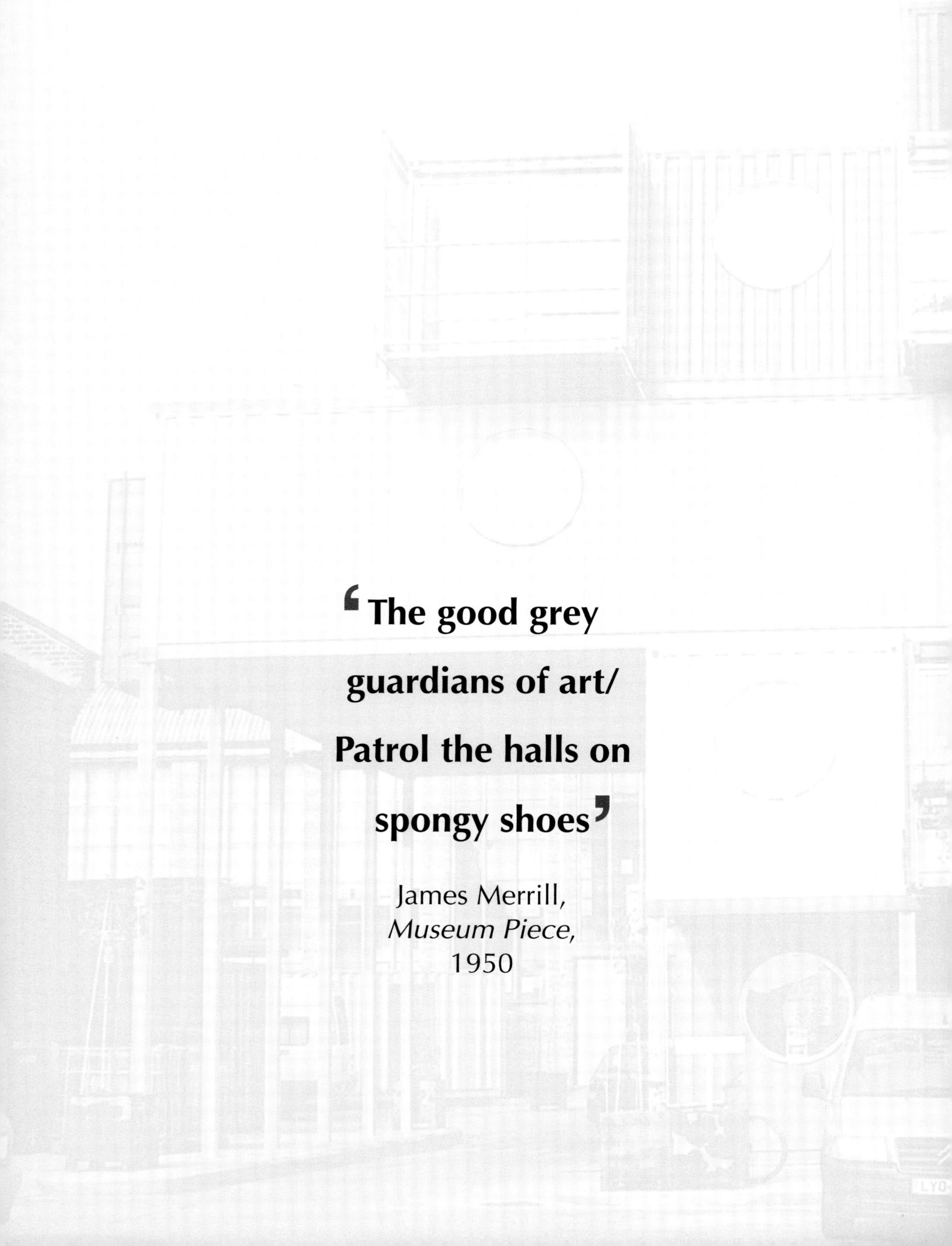

'The good grey
guardians of art/
Patrol the halls on
spongy shoes'

James Merrill,
Museum Piece,
1950

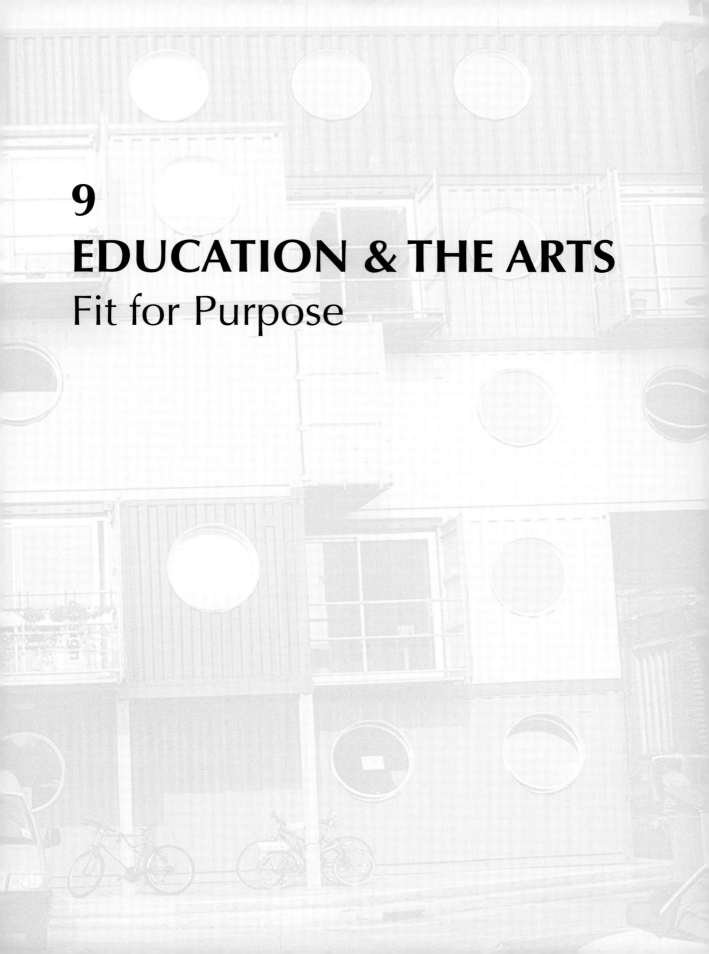

9
EDUCATION & THE ARTS
Fit for Purpose

COLLEGE OF ARMS

QUEEN VICTORIA STREET, EC4

For anyone who is a sucker for pageantry, it is hard to resist the allure of somebody sporting a scarlet and gold tabard and calling himself Rouge Dragon, Bluemantle, Portcullis, Norroy (or 'north king') and Ulster, or most definitely Garter King of Arms. As Officers of Arms the gentlemen in question occupy this building, and having been granted their first charter as heralds by the last of the Plantagenet kings, Richard III, in 1484, they were initially active as a kind of 'snobbery police' charged with preventing social climbing peacocks from outranking themselves with undeserved displays of colour, beast and symbol. These days, however, they confine themselves to examining and recording pedigrees, the granting of arms and, under the Duke of Norfolk as hereditary Earl Marshal, arranging coronations, the State Opening of Parliament and other important state occasions.

Until receiving Richard's charter the kings, heralds and pursuivants who make up the College (in the sense of a body of colleagues) formed part of the royal household. In 1484 they were presented with their own premises in Upper Thames Street, a substantial house known as Coldharbour, from which they were ousted by Henry VII after the Battle of Bosworth Field the following year. In 1555 his granddaughter Mary Tudor granted them a new charter, however, and gave them the late fifteenth-century Derby House on the present site close to Paul's Wharf, although like Coldharbour this was lost in the Great Fire.

Luckily the library with its irreplaceable records, rolls and charters was saved and in 1678 Maurice Emmet, Master Bricklayer to the Office of Works, completed the present building to a design by the Lancaster Herald. By some miracle (and a change of wind) it survived the Blitz in May 1941, even though two churches, one either side, were razed to the ground.

Overlooked by giant Ionic pilasters, the courtyard to the street is largely Emmet's own (some alterations were made in order to widen the street) but the splendid wrought-iron gates were presented by a grateful American benefactor in the mid-1950s. Having come originally from Goodrich Court in Herefordshire, this generous gift from Mr Blevins Davis replaced those taken for scrap during the war.

Plain, unfortunately situated perhaps, but undeniably magnificent, the College of Arms is sadly not open to the public. However, for a fee anyone can have what the twentieth-century author and diarist James Lees-Milne described as this 'dry assembly of dessicated, hirsute pedants' research his or her genealogy, or establish whether or not armorial bearings already exist in the family and if not petition the College for a Grant of Arms of their own.

It's an expensive business, though, as the pedants' learning and expertise are considerable. But for the peacocks it is a harmless bit of fun, and in practice few if any are refused permission to add his or her name to the ranks of the armigerous (nor, once new arms have been granted, to apply them to anything from a car door – in lieu of a carriage – to the pocket of their pyjamas).

CONTAINER CITY

ORCHARD PLACE, E14

Creating a uniquely colourful arts, residential and community centre using old sea containers, this imaginative exercise in recycling is situated across the river from the Millennium Dome at Leamouth. As such it continues a maritime tradition which for more than 200 years has seen this area of east London active in the manufacture of buoys, docking equipment and in particular lightships.

Following the decline of most marine and manufacturing activities along this stretch of the Thames, a competition was held to decide what to do with the large number of often quite attractive listed buildings in the area. Eventually the London Docklands Development Corporation selected a highly creative outfit called Urban Space Management which had a plan to develop this particular site, called Trinity Buoy Wharf, as a cultural centre for the arts with artists' studios, workshops and exhibition spaces.

An important part of the USM proposal was to build the arts centre using recycled metal shipping containers, a solution which kept costs to a minimum and allowed for extremely rapid construction. In all, thirty self-contained workspaces were planned, to be built in two phases and called Container City 1 and Container City 2. The containers were stacked five storeys high in an attractively complex arrangement whereby some overhanging boxes would be supported on secondary steel framing to make space for vehicles to pass beneath.

Fitted with large sliding windows and pivoting portholes, and sprayed with insulation to prevent the build-up of condensation, a single 8ft × 8ft × 40ft container, said USM, would suffice for a small studio or office. However, a key component of the concept was to ensure that the boxes interconnected in such a way as to allow for a variety of different interiors with a great degree of flexibility.

As a prototype the design must surely prove a winner, a concept which makes even more sense as the global stockpile of disused containers continues to grow. Cheap, durable and extremely strong despite walls just 2mm thick, the 4-ton containers are also long-lasting and designed to be readily transportable. Able to be installed rapidly and at a very low initial cost – less than half the cost of conventional construction, say USM – when brightly painted they are also cheerfully funky. Little wonder then that already the idea has been used to create offices, workshops, modish live–work modules, even a pre-school nursery in Harlesden, north London. Being able to support ten times their own weight when stacked, such constructions require very little in the way of foundations and, stacked on end, the containers can even be used to create stair and lift towers while balconies can be fashioned from the disused doors.

CURATOR'S HOUSE

GOUGH SQUARE, EC4

As the name suggests this tiny, curious two-door hideaway was originally built for the guardian of Dr Samuel Johnson's famous house at No. 17. Today this corner of the square (which is actually more of an L-shape) is one of the more charming reminders of the days when the streets around the Fleet river were characterised by a glorious if confusing profusion of tiny backwaters, closed courts and narrow alleyways.

Traditionally occupied by the journalists, writers and lawyers with whom this area has long been associated, too many of these ancient thoroughfares have since been lost to rapacious City developers. For this reason Gough Square is rather special, managing to convey a sense of what the old City must have been like even though Johnson's house is the only actual survivor from the original seventeenth-century plan.

Part of its appeal depends on several of these old alleyways still winding their way into and around it. Thus narrow conduits such as Hind, Bolt, St Dunstan's and, inevitably perhaps, Johnson's, Courts – although this last one was named not for the great imbiber and lexicographer but after an otherwise forgotten tailor – still echo to the noises of the past and provide those visitors who come on foot with some much needed relief from the bland high-rise, hi-tech monoliths of the modern business environment.

Dr Johnson himself, despite supplying future anthologists with perhaps the most often repeated quotation about London life, was not a local lad. He arrived here in 1737, having shared a single horse for the journey from Lichfield with his friend and pupil, the actor David Garrick. Once here, though, he moved around a lot, Boswell listing no fewer than seventeen different addresses for him of which this is the only one left standing. At a rent of £30 a year he took the house from 1748 until 1759, which is to say before he actually met Boswell. The reason he chose it was to be close to his printer, William Strahan. However, plenty of note happened to him during the time, including the death of his beloved wife and the completion of his great work, the *Dictionary*, in which he was assisted by six clerks beavering away in this very attic.

The survival of what is now the only Grade I domestic building in the City of London owes more to good fortune, however, than it does to national respect for our mother tongue. Not just because it was so badly bombed at least three times during the 1940s – fortunately members of the Auxiliary Fire Service were camping out in the house at the time, but charred beams can still be seen in the attic – but also because, after an unhappy spell when No. 17 was being used as a cheap hotel, it was acquired by the well-disposed Cecil Harmsworth. A member of the Northcliffe-Rothermere newspaper-owning dynasty, he bought it only because he happened to be strolling by when the For Sale boards went up in 1910. The price he paid is rumoured to have been £3,500, and it was he who restored it and built this little curator's dwelling alongside before opening Dr Johnson's House to the public in 1914.

HORNIMAN MUSEUM

100 LONDON ROAD, SE23

Their collections usually neither specialised nor local and access or parking often a problem, it is all too easy to forget the many museums and galleries found in London's suburbs. That said, of course, this at least means that when one does visit such places the crowds are mostly, happily, somewhere else. Fronting on to the South Circular the Horniman is one of the better examples, presented to the people of London by Quaker tea magnate and Liberal MP Frederick John Horniman (1835–1906) along with 16 acres of parkland with views towards the Home Counties. Entry is free, as indeed is declared, in words carved in stone, on the outside of the building.

Although it has been added to since, when he made the bequest in 1901 this was very much the collection of just one man. Covering all aspects of ethnography and animal evolution, these more than 250,000 specimens from nature now include everything from fossilised footprints of the iguanadon discovered at Swanage in Dorset to a working glass beehive in which the active inhabitants can be observed going about their labours. What is more (and unlike Augustus Henry Lane Fox Pitt-Rivers at Oxford), being a keen traveller Horniman collected the vast majority of the original exhibits himself.

Together with Indian sculpture, exotic bronzes from Benin, axes and many magic and ritual objects from around the world – another 60,000 pieces in all – Horniman originally displayed this fascinating assemblage at his home, Surrey House, which together with the gardens were opened to the public three days a week from Christmas Eve 1890. Later the Carse Collection of musical instruments was presented to the museum and, now numbering some 6,500 different examples from every period of history and all corners of the Earth, this is held to be the finest such collection in the world.

In 1898 the decision was taken to demolish Surrey House whereupon Horniman commissioned the architect of the Whitechapel Gallery, Charles Harrison Townsend, to produce one of the best public buildings of this period. A boldly decorated and highly original art nouveau design, of stone and red brick, its most distinctive features are an immense barrel-vaulted roof over the main hall, the dominating clock tower and the attractive allegorical murals of *Humanity in the House of Circumstance* by R. Anning Bell.

With the emphasis on dramatic curves and buttressing, and strong horizontal banding, Townsend clearly drew on his earlier work at Whitechapel. However, other, more unusual, features such as the immense tower and its radiused corners, the canopies over the clock faces and the four strange circular pinnacles made the Horniman if anything even more successful. One of south London's most original buildings, as clever as it is charming, it is also a perfect period piece despite suffering a variety of more recent additions.

LEIGHTON HOUSE MUSEUM

HOLLAND PARK ROAD, W14

Denied access as we now are to Halsey Ricardo's fabulous Debenham House (q.v.), a brisk stroll round the corner to the former home of the painter and sculptor Lord Leighton (1830–96) is probably the next best thing. Not that one would think so looking at its simple red-brick exterior, but like a freshly mined geode whose outer shell is cracked open by the geologist's hammer to reveal the glittering, iridescent interior of purple amethyst or celestite, here the discreet and mannered appearance of a prosperous west London house conceals an interior of wondrous eastern splendour.

That said, when it was built in the 1860s George Aitchison's classical exterior would have been considered highly unusual even without reference to its interior appointments. Certainly, built very much according to Lord Leighton's own ideas, it still looks markedly different from the other artists' houses in the neighbourhood such as those in Melbury Road belonging to G.F. Watts, Luke Fildes, Holman Hunt and Marcus Stone. More than anything, it was redolent of an Italianate villa, as perhaps one might expect from many of Frederick Leighton's paintings, and indeed some of the original interior decoration of ebony woodwork and red walls had a distinctly Venetian character. But the real clue to the exotic nature of the interior was not built until much later, in about 1877, when Aitchison was commissioned to add the so-called Arab Hall in which Leighton wished to display his extensive collection of rare Islamic tiles.

Aitchison based his design on Palermo's twelfth-century Muslim Palace of La Zisa, using drawings he had completed while travelling through Moorish Europe, and from the street the giveaway is the dome, modestly proportioned but still a surprising thing to see in W14. It isn't until you go inside, however, that the true pleasures of this remarkable house, and the brilliance of Aitchison's design, become wholly apparent.

Step in off the pavement and beneath the dome is a truly magical scene: a black marble pool with a fountain gently playing above a geometric mosaic floor; the late summer sun streaming in through coloured lights and elaborate latticework shutters; and red marble pillars topped with gold capitals to provide a stunning contrast with the tile-covered walls of antique blue and white from Cairo, Damascus and Rhodes. These sixteenth- and seventeenth-century tiles, collected over many years by Leighton and two roving friends, Sir Richard Burton and the antiquarian Sir Caspar Purdon Clarke, are supplemented by more recent designs from William de Morgan, just one of the many artists who worked on the house under the careful direction of Aitchison and his knowledgeable client.

Success for Leighton had of course come early: he was still in his twenties when his Cimabue's *Madonna Carried in Procession Through Florence* was bought by Queen Victoria for an incredible 600 guineas. Thus, when he first conceived this house he was a very wealthy young man with no plans to marry. Aitchison's original plan was therefore modest, with just a drawing room on the ground floor and a studio and one bedroom above. As Leighton's standing grew – first a knight, then a baronet, later President of the Royal Academy, and finally, on his deathbed, the first English artist to be made a peer – so the house grew with him. Even Leighton himself apparently referred to his house as his autobiography and now, an exemplar of High Victorian aesthetics, the place still functions to give one the most perfect impression of the wealth, status and sensibilities of a leading artist of the period.

ORION GRADUATE CENTRE

HOLLOWAY ROAD, N7

Daniel Libeskind's dramatic exercise in extravagant postmodernism was completed in 2004 and, standing in such strong contrast to its otherwise extremely dreary surroundings, works very successfully as a bold advertisement for one of Britain's youngest universities. Despite being a relatively small building, it has been described by the architect himself as a major gateway to the university, the building's name – describing the spatial emblem of the northern sky – suggests, he says, 'a guiding light for developing a unique icon for the London Metropolitan University on Holloway Road'.

Certainly, though cash-strapped as presumably all such establishments now are, the university must have decided that this sort of landmark architecture by one of the big, globe-striding names would reap some long-term benefits in terms of attracting new talent. Indeed, its creator even refers to it as being like a magnet to the facility. 'Buildings', he says, 'should not be just factories for knowledge but have an interesting atmosphere [where] students and teachers should have some fun.'

Comprising three dramatically intersecting blocks clad in coloured, embossed stainless steel, the building looks almost as though three giant metal boxes had been hurled into the ground. Certainly the strange angles and leaning walls which result from such a design are quite vertigo-inducing once you enter its simple but striking interior. Doorways, huge geometric windows, even the lecture halls, cafeteria and galleries are all completely irregular in shape and orientation, while twisted staircases make a dizzying ascent with the exterior walls actually leaning in over the handrails. The fact that everything here is wonky (as at his similarly zinc-clad Jewish Museum in Berlin, and closer to home the Imperial War Museum North) posed a few interesting engineering problems too. Thus the blinds, for example, which are clearly needed with such large areas of glazing, require a complex system of pulleys and guidewires in order to ensure that they remain parallel to the windows and function correctly rather than just hanging uselessly over the pavement outside.

For obvious reasons the three cleverly intersecting elements which make up the Graduate Centre lack the powerful, almost overwhelming, symbolism of the Berlin museum. Nonetheless they are arranged in an attempt to emphasise the building's multiple functions, one making a connection with the public passing by outside and the other university buildings behind, another to the nearby tube station (a more obvious connection with the rest of the world), and the last block placing the building in context with the street on which it stands. That final point is important, for Libeskind clearly always wanted his building to have 'an enlivening impact on the wider urban context . . . a contribution to the intense urban life on Holloway Road and to the graduate students of the London Metropolitan University'. In this regard local residents seem to like it, none of those questioned objecting to its deliberately weird and uncompromising appearance, something which might not have been the case had such a design been offered for a central or more obviously prestigious site than this grimy through-route in north London.

More than anything, though, with its shining and ever-changing surface, the £3 million building makes a bold, confident statement and does so in an area crying out for something remarkable. It is also good to see a Libeskind permanently installed in London, and an educational establishment once more offering the public architecture which is something other than merely functional.

THE ROUNDHOUSE

CHALK FARM ROAD, NW1

Hugely appealing but relatively space inefficient and often quite impractical, round buildings rarely seem to work as well as one hopes and as a consequence are particularly scarce in expensive urban areas. North London's most famous and distinctive arts venue has the advantage of having been built for a different purpose, namely as part of London's Victorian railway network. Completed in 1847 to the designs of (George) Stephenson, Dockwray & Normanville, it originally housed a turntable to turn locomotives of the London & Birmingham Railway, along with winding gear and a stationary steam engine, which were used to winch trains up the steep hill from Euston station. From Camden, with the gradient flattening out, conventional steam power was able to do the rest.

Its life on the working railway was to be shortlived, however. By 1869, 160ft in diameter and with a vast roof supported on twenty-four cast iron columns, it was no longer suited to its original purpose and, converted to a warehouse and factory, was thereafter connected with the production of Gilbey's Gin before that company's move in 1963 to Harlow in Essex.

Though listed as a building of architectural and historic interest, by 1964 it was disused, drafty and dilapidated when playwright Arnold Wesker and his Centre 42 moved in. Taking its name from Resolution 42 of the annual conference of the Trades Union Congress – calling for the unions to be more involved in the arts – and very much involved in the concept of 'art for everyone', Centre 42 organised festivals around the country until the leaseholders of the Roundhouse offered the building as a permanent home.

The scene was thus set for one of London's more unusual buildings to become the leading rock venue of the 1960s, kicking off on 15 October 1966 with a concert by Syd Barrett and Pink Floyd to mark the launch of the radical underground paper *International Times*. The building also briefly hosted the legendary UFO Club (at which the house bands were Soft Machine and the Floyd) when its original home was closed by the police. Then came the Rolling Stones, along with Jimi Hendrix, Led Zeppelin, and even the Doors, who played their only UK gig here. In the latter part of the 1970s punk rockers also made their presence felt before the venue finally closed its doors again in 1983.

With a question mark once more appearing over the future of this unique structure, a charity called The Roundhouse Trust was established in 1998 with plans to reopen the Roundhouse as 'a flexible and adaptable performance space'. Now, with room inside for 1,700 seated, or nearly twice that number standing, the trustees plan a programme of work reflecting the excitement and diversity of the arts in the twenty-first century. With plans to include a wide range of the performing arts such as music, theatre, dance, circus and digital media, the programme should facilitate the long-overdue return of the Roundhouse to London's thriving cultural life.

ROYAL COLLEGE OF ORGANISTS

KENSINGTON GORE, SW7

When one reads that 'across the road, in the smoke-filled male-dominated Kensington Gore clubhouse of the then ultra-stuffy Royal College of Organists, men in dark suits and port-stained college ties must have been choking on their pipes . . .', it is hard to reconcile this vision of misogynistic clubmen with the slightly feminine cream, pale blue and maroon colour scheme which decorates the outside of the building in question.

Somewhat surprising too to think that, with its fussy detailing and busy *sgraffito* or incised plasterwork façade, it was designed by a soldier, a Royal Engineer named Lieutenant H.H. Cole. He was the son of Henry Cole, the first director of the South Kensington Museum (now the Victoria and Albert), and prior to that a major driving force behind the Great Exhibition and the creation of 'Albertopolis' with the many national institutions, colleges and museums, some of which are still located in this part of London today.

Set amid the Classical, Renaissance and Dutch Revival-style buildings of Albertopolis, this particular building with its unique decoration was originally conceived not for organists at all but for musicians in general. This perhaps explains why a careful scrutiny of F.W. Moody's monumental frieze today reveals plenty of musicians but no actual organists. Instead, when completed in 1876 it was for the National Training School for Music, an establishment founded after an unfavourable 1866 report by the Society of Arts on the state of musical education in England.

Once the foundation stone had been laid by the Duke of Edinburgh in 1873, Lt Cole explained that, 'after mature consideration and consultation it was decided that the style of architecture to be adopted . . . should be as different from that of the Royal Albert Hall as to provoke no comparison unfavourable with the school'. He needn't have worried since the presence of the hall, the creation of yet another Royal Engineer, Captain Fowke, simply adds to the confusion of constrasting styles in an area which includes the nearby Albert Court mansion flats, Richard Norman Shaw's pseudo-country house (Lowther Lodge, now the Royal Geographical Society), and most obviously the Royal College of Arts with its dark and brutally modern eight-storey teaching block.

In any event the school was to be short-lived. With its first Principal the composer Sir Arthur Sullivan (1842–1900), by 1883 the National Training School had been superceded by the Royal College of Music. In 1904 the organists moved into the building thus vacated (having hitherto met at the Bloomsbury home of their founder, Richard Davidge Limpus) before removing to St Andrew's Holborn upon the expiration of their lease in the 1980s, and then to Sir Nicholas Grimshaw's massive Millennium Point development in Birmingham.

TRINITY BUOY WHARF LIGHTHOUSE

ORCHARD PLACE, E14

London has a surprising number of windmills, several folly towers, even the remains of a semaphore tower or two, but only one genuine lighthouse and that's this well-preserved example. Now part of a unique arts experiment, it has dominated Trinity Buoy Wharf at Leamouth since 1864. Unusually, given its position right on the river, it was never intended to perform the usual navigational functions but rather to enable the Corporation of Trinity House to carry out experiments needed to develop the lighting for its working lighthouses and lightships.

In fact when it was completed there was already one on the site, built a decade earlier by Trinity House's scientific adviser, Sir Michael Faraday. He used it to pioneer various advances in electric lighting which in turn were put into practice at Kent's South Foreland Lighthouse. Sadly, Faraday's tower was eventually dismantled in the 1920s.

The surviving lighthouse was designed by Sir James Nicholas Douglass. The chief engineer to the corporation, he was responsible for designing almost two dozen other lighthouses including those at Gun Fleet Pile and Wolf Rock as well as the most famous one on Eddystone in 1882. Like its predecessor, the London lighthouse was used to test and perfect various different lanterns, with the adjoining low-rise building being used by Faraday as a workshop where he worked on a number of advanced lens designs. Thereafter, and indeed until the middle of the twentieth century, a new role was found for the lighthouse, which functioned as a training base for lighthouse keepers. While they were schooled in all aspects of navigational lighting and optics, the tower itself was employed for testing lamps which were viewed from across the river at Shooters Hill.

Since New Year's Day 2000, however, the lighthouse has enjoyed a fresh life as home to 'Longplayer', a unique sound installation by Artangel and Jem Finer. Based on a piece of music twenty minutes long and played on Tibetan singing bowls, the performance is controlled by a sophisticated computer program which, by minutely varying the music and ensuring that no sequence or segment is ever repeated, aims to play the piece for 1,000 years. This makes it the world's longest musical composition as well as one of the strangest of millennium projects.

'Industry without art is brutality'

John Ruskin,
a lecture on art,
1870

10
FORM & FUNCTION
Working Buildings

THE ARK

HAMMERSMITH FLYOVER, W6

Now somewhat eclipsed by the Swiss Re Building, otherwise known as the Gherkin (q.v.), for most Londoners the general awareness of the new vogue for unorthodox shapes in building design probably started with the Ark, a strange glass helmet of a building which hovers darkly over this busy and unpleasant corner of west London. A highly original and generally very popular landmark, Ralph Erskine's 1992 copper and brown glass block looks from some angles like a globe or an orb but is in reality a considerably more complex shape. Squeezed on to a cramped and unpromising site, its unusual contours enable it to shield a generous south-facing atrium behind nine storeys of offices overlooking the road thundering in from Heathrow Airport but without dominating the lower buildings in its lee.

Hemmed in by a concrete flyover on one side and a railway cutting on another, its characteristic shape arises from a relatively narrow base which is situated way below the level of the A4. This flares out to produce a series of generous deck spaces – the parallels with an ocean-going vessel are unavoidable – with these being supported on brick-clad concrete columns hidden beneath the waterline (as it were) and so invisible to passing motorists. Inside the Ark the nautical theme continues with its bright, white-painted bulkheads, teak decking and tiny portholes. Indeed, there is even a so-called crow's nest on the summit, a strange little annexe crowning the more than 4,500 glass panels and 1,500 sun-sensitive blinds which give form to the finished building.

The Ark's glass construction and its eccentric shape make its actual size very hard to determine. With a height of 250ft at its tallest point it is a surprisingly large building, and it has five storeys even on its lower side, where the design has been scaled down so as not to tower over the more domestic streetscape and hospital. Inside too one gets little idea of its true size, the total volume being broken up by many staggered floors, suspended walkways and a bewildering array of terraces, balconies and meeting areas, all arranged around the luxuriously large, airy atrium.

Designed to provide unique and flexible office accommodation – since losing the original occupier, the drinks multinational Seagram, it has been let to a number of smaller tenants – the Ark was one of the pioneers of the concept of the office as a community. The focus therefore is very much on the natural light-filled central atrium, a common area which provides space not just for the usual office-support facilities but also a fitness and lifestyle centre, a bar and restaurant and shared conference facilities. At the same time a white noise system generates a continuous, low-frequency hiss which, it is claimed, helps people to concentrate. Described as 'calming' by first-time visitors to the Ark, it means occupants can play music in their own areas without disturbing adjacent working groups.

Sadly, though, one particularly striking external feature of the original design has been abandoned, namely a large ramp leading up to the entrance which would have provided authentically ark-like access to this unique building. A cutaway in the façade perhaps shows where such a ramp would have been folded into the 'hull' once the two-by-twos were all on board, but in the end practical considerations intervened and it was left out.

BERRY BROS & RUDD

3 ST JAMES'S STREET, SW1

The oldest shop in England actually sells hats: Nelson himself called on James Lock & Co. to pay his bills before leaving London for the last time, and it was here that the Duke of Wellington bought that distinctive plumed hat which he wore at Waterloo. However, the wine trade runs it pretty close for only a very few years behind, and indeed only a step or two along the pavement, Berry Brothers & Rudd is one of the capital's hidden treasures.

This area of St James's was presented by Charles II to a loyal courtier, one Henry Jermyn, Earl of St Albans, and it was he who developed these empty fields into what is now a rich and exclusive enclave hidden from the throng and vulgar hubbub of Oxford Street and Piccadilly Circus. Against all odds but assisted by some valuable freeholds it has survived to a great degree, successfully retaining an air of an otherwise vanished and largely masculine world of clubs and claret, bespoke shirt and bootmakers, swordsmiths and cigars. And the Berry family have been at its heart almost from the start, having been 'established in XVIIth Century' as the simple yet elegant signwriting on its front attests.

Backing on to a narrow stone-flagged, gas-lit courtyard – called Pickering Place and entered through a delightful half-timbered passage where two young blades reputedly fought London's last recorded duel – the company's early eighteenth-century building stands on the sight of an old coffee house whose sign still hangs above the door. Sadly there is no longer any trace of its predecessor, the farmhouse of Henry Jermyn's day, but with sloping wooden floors, ramshackle Victorian furniture, Arts and Crafts trappings, displays of antique glassware and darkly panelled walls, the present premises look for all the world more like a careful recreation than a thriving, commercial concern.

But then the shopkeepers in this part of town have always had a particularly fine sense of history. For example, when Westminster Abbey needed a new hat for its wax effigy of Nelson they sent to James Lock which naturally still had his Lordship's measurements on file in records it has kept since about 1700. Similarly at Berry Brothers, an eighth-generation family concern, they continue to refer to the giant leather-bound ledgers containing the personal details of distinguished customers such as Lord Byron, Beau Brummel, George IV, King Louis-Philippe and Napoleon III. The shop also houses an immense pair of balance scales, a contraption which has been used since 1765 to weigh celebrated visitors to the elegant glass-fronted premises.

Best of all, however, are the Berry Brother cellars, quarried over the centuries, a small portion of which are these days used for tastings and private or corporate dinners. As for the remainder, extending as far down the street as Pall Mall and beneath the courtyard, they explain how it is that such a small shop can straightaway meet almost any order. With a stock approaching 250,000 bottles, some dating from as early as the 1830s, Berry Bros & Rudd is for the oenophile an authentic Aladdin's Cave.

CITY HALL

THE QUEEN'S WALK, SE1

Part of 'More London', the massive, modishly named waterside development at the southern foot of Tower Bridge, the Greater London Authority's headquarters is together with the spiralling cost of driving into central London perhaps the most visible sign of Mayor Ken Livingstone's return to power. Dominating a 13-acre building plot, and directly opposite a World Heritage site, an eye-catching, landmark building was clearly necessary. To this end Foster & Partners proposed a distinctive glass globe to house an assembly chamber and offices spread over ten storeys. Built around a mammoth 2,100 ton steel skeleton, and completed on time and to budget, the site and the design we see now were both chosen from more than fifty different proposals.

For Lord Foster it is very much a case of advancing themes he had explored earlier in his Reichstag project. Using huge expanses of glass to express the transparency and accessibility of the democratic process – the debating chamber faces north across the river so Londoners can see the Assembly at work – City Hall also demonstrates the potential for more sustainable and less polluting public buildings.

The shape itself, variously described as a geometrically modified sphere or Red Ken's glass testicle, was created in order to minimise the surface area exposed to direct sunlight, just one of a number of features incorporated into the design to make the building as green as possible. To achieve this last point an analysis was made of sunlight patterns throughout the year, the resulting thermal map of the building's surface determining the choice of cladding. At the same time the building was designed to lean back to the south, thereby providing shade for offices inside.

As a result, claims the GLA, its new home runs on a quarter of the energy consumed by a comparable high-specification office building of a more conventional design. This, they say, has been achieved by using several ecologically sound, passive environmental control systems as well as by adopting this radical form and geometry. For example, by deriving the basic shape from a sphere, which has approximately 20 per cent less surface area than a cube of a similar volume, the building's designers have been able to reduce both solar gain and heat loss throughout the year. Similarly, further green gains have been made by recycling the considerable heat generated by computers and electric lighting, and by making it possible for the offices to be naturally ventilated (installing windows which actually open). In addition cold groundwater is used to provide air-conditioning for the building, this being extracted from the water table through two bore holes and later used to flush the loos once it has been used to cool the structure.

Rising from the entrance foyer, gentle ramps allow visitors to move through the building, while a versatile public space on the top floor – called London's Living Room – is used for exhibitions and functions with unparalleled views out across the City. Outside, a large public area called the Scoop further underlines this theme of greater access to the general public. Situated to the west of the building, this elegant sunken oval amphitheatre of grey limestone can seat up to a thousand people for organised events such as lunchtime concerts and evening drama. For the rest of the time, and with a curving ramp and steep steps linking it to the improved riverside walkway, it provides a modern, elegant interpretation of a traditional piazza.

COTTAGE ORNÉ
SOHO SQUARE, W1

The gardeners of London really do rather nicely for themselves when it comes to finding somewhere to store their forks or shelter from the weather when it's time for a cup of tea. In Lower Grosvenor Gardens, given to the City of Westminster by its titular duke, they have the use of a delightful shell-encrusted folly, one of a pair presented to London by the French government in memory of Marshal Foch. Similarly those responsible for the day-to-day maintenance of the gardens in St James's Square (still technically private, though with provision for daytime public access) enjoy a little summerhouse, this one designed by John Nash and given by another duke, Northumberland. Perhaps the most extraordinary of London's potting sheds, however, is this one in Soho Square.

Thought to have been designed by S.J. Thacker, central London's only *cottage orné* was completed in 1876 and, though dismissed by Nikolaus Pevsner as 'silly', the little timbered octagon provides a central focus, not to mention a certain curiosity value, to these otherwise rather unremarkable gardens. It has its origins in a much larger one, namely a house constructed for himself on the south side of the square by the Duke of Monmouth (1649–85), eldest of Charles II's illegitimate children.

Once acknowledged as a son of the King, Monmouth planned a magnificent London palace with a street front of 76ft, a depth of 280ft and extensive stabling and coach houses running along the east side of Frith Street. Work on it started in February 1682, but in the event the Duke did not live to see the building finished, still less to enjoy it, once his estates and later his life were forfeited to the Crown. (Falling foul of his father after being implicated with other potential regicides in the Rye House Plot of 1683, the Duke escaped execution and fled to the Low Countries. Returning to engage in rebellion two years later, however, he was less fortunate and met his end after the Battle of Sedgemoor on 5 July 1685, his battle-cry on the field being a shout of 'so-ho'.)

At that time the square was called King rather than Soho, although it is still unclear whether this was after Monmouth's natural father or a local genealogist called King who claimed to have designed the layout. Certainly there was a statue of the king there, by William III's sculptor-in-ordinary, the Dane Caius Gabriel Cibber, although this was later removed to the garden of Royal Academician Frederick Goodall together with a large fountain. The fountain, boasting four jets representing the Thames, Severn, Humber and Tyne rivers, was never returned. Instead its place was taken by Thacker's 'silly' summer house, just one of a series of expensive improvements paid for by the square's inhabitants who well into the late nineteenth century were still refusing to allow the public into what remained their private gardens.

In 1938 Cibber's statue did come back from Harrow Weald, however, via the widow of the librettist W.S. Gilbert. Unfortunately now somewhat battered and much corroded by the London air (sufficiently battered to have been mistaken for the Duke, that is), without its fountain the effect is somewhat less impressive than the sculptor might have wished.

CREWE HOUSE

CURZON STREET, SW1

While ranked after St James's and Belgravia, Mayfair has never lost its position as one of London's very smartest addresses, yet even in its heyday it would not have had too many detached dwellings quite as large and as grand as Crewe House. Nor would many of those that once graced its streets have been sufficiently set back from the road to allow for a sweeping carriage drive quite like this one. Today there is little comparable to the house anywhere north of Piccadilly – arguably nothing save Lord Palmerston's noble dwelling, the erstwhile home of the Naval and Military Club at No. 94 – and while the almost too-pristine finish of its gleaming cream stucco exterior can occasionally make the whole confection seem a little artificial, the Marquess of Crewe's immense private palace is most definitely the genuine, late Georgian article.

It was built in about 1730 by the noted architect and builder Edward Shepherd. That's Mr Shepherd of Shepherd Market, the still charming series of little byways he planned over the way to service his aristocratic clients. His work was, however, substantially altered and aggrandised in about 1813 before being acquired by the first Lord Wharncliffe. With the additions of various columns, two pretty wings and a substantial central pediment, the simplicity of Shepherd's original 'white garden house' was to some extent lost to a more obvious idea of expensive Georgian grandeur. Today passers-by can marvel at Crewe's striking seven-bay front with its two and a half storeys, the whole effect beautifully set off by those matching bow-fronted wings looking out over the emerald green of what, rated per square foot, must be one of London's most valuable front gardens. Indeed, even in the country such a vision would be quite an eye-catcher; and in the centre of town – and especially at night when it is floodlit – it seems almost too good to be true.

In a sense it is precisely that, for while the thought of it as a museum or gallery like Hertford House in Manchester Square is appealing, Crewe House is emphatically not open to the public and can only be admired by peering from the pavement through the immaculate railings. The good news at least is that, unlike so many other great London houses, this one has survived both commercial usage and the public sector, most recently as the headquarters of the Thomas Tilling Group of Companies and before that when it was home to the Ministry of Propaganda.

Now, though, it has a quite different role again, as the embassy of the kingdom of Saudi Arabia. The freehold is said to have cost King Fahd a hefty £37 million – and this was in the 1980s when money was still money – while Lord Crewe had paid a mere £90,000 for it less than a century before. Inevitably the sale caused some upset at the time, notably among local residents who feared for the survival of this unique slice of their Mayfair 'village'. But their concerns now seem unfounded and the survival of Crewe House – gloriously intact, monumental, and as eye-stopping as ever – seems for the present to be safe.

C. HOARE & CO.

37 FLEET STREET, EC4

Anyone lucky enough to enjoy a private tour of Blenheim Palace may get the chance to weigh in his hands the magnificent brass key to the front door. At C. Hoare & Co. in Fleet Street, however, there is no need for such a thing. Its front door can be locked only from the inside because, night and day, 365 days a year, and for more than 300 years, at least one of the partners has always been on the premises to slide the bolt across. It has been that way since 1672, when Richard Hoare, a goldsmith and banker, founded the company. Today, an eleventh-generation family concern, C. Hoare & Co. is run by no fewer than nine of his direct descendants.

Originally trading on Cheapside 'at the sign of the Golden Bottle', Britain's oldest surviving private bank moved to Fleet Street in 1690, since when its clients have included Catherine of Braganza, Gainsborough, Chippendale, Byron, 'Beau' Nash, Pepys, Dryden and John Evelyn. Mostly the bank has thrived by staying small and exclusive while its rivals have sold out, gone for growth or simply gone to the wall. The fate of Barings, for example, is well known. Even older than Hoare's, Child & Co. like Drummonds went to the Royal Bank of Scotland. Similarly, when Coutts came under the wing of NatWest first the frock coats went out of the door and then the family which had until then held on to the management reins. In fact, more than a few of the founding Money-Coutts family went straight to Hoare's, joining the mere 10,000 other customers who are fortunate enough to bank at 37 Fleet Street. Still welcomed in by a doorman sporting a frock coat, even today customers are hand-picked as carefully as the members of a private club. (Requiring references from two established customers, there is no guarantee of entry even for offspring of families with a long history of banking there.) Unsurprisingly, and while admitting they have fewer landowners on board than they once had, the partners refuse to confirm whether or not their number includes any lottery winners or footballers, although at least one car dealer is known to be among them.

As for the building, it is relatively modern, having been built for the bank in 1829 by Charles Parker. Its basement incorporates part of the cellars of an Elizabethan tavern, the Mitre, but with its panelled walls, stone-flagged hallway and high mahogany and brass counters it is otherwise very much of its era. Even so, in much the same way that these historic surroundings conceal what is clearly a thoroughly modern and highly sophisticated banking operation, the central stove of cast iron no longer heats the hall, having been superseded by a more modern system which is carefully hidden.

Such techniques of progress through stealth are obviously critical in a business which though fond of tradition cannot afford to be sentimental. After all, when the Hoares moved into their new building England had close to 4,000 private banks; now this is the sole survivor. Nor was the Hoares' own survival ever certain, particularly during the mid-nineteenth-century when a row blew up between the principal partners. One was Low Church, apparently, and the other High, and wishing not to meet each other they agreed to take it in turns to run the bank. With each being in charge for a six-month period, the business somehow survived. Even so, it is to be hoped that should a similar set of circumstances arise 150 years later the present partners – all cousins, fourth cousins and ninth cousins – would find a more sensible arrangement.

LIBERTY'S

GREAT MARLBOROUGH STREET, W1

'Wrong', 'wrong' and 'wrongest of all' – Nikolaus Pevsner was understandably no lover of mock-Tudor in general and Liberty's in particular. However, the West End's most famous piece of stockbroker Tudor remains one of the few structures anyone notices around Oxford Street and Regent Street and to its credit it is at least created using materials with some provenance. One says that because while the building is clearly a fake, and a fake which contrasts horribly with the Classical façade of its other half as well as with the black and gilt of the nearby Palladium, the timbers used by architects E.S. & E.T. Hall are more than mere stick-ons and indeed came from two genuine Royal Navy men-o'-war. The tiles for the roof are hand-made too, while the leaded windows really are leaded – but then perhaps this is only to be expected given Arthur Lazenby Liberty's pre-eminent role in furthering the cause of his beloved Arts and Crafts Society.

After an apprenticeship with the wonderful-sounding Farmer & Rogers Great Cloak and Shawl Emporium, and having been inspired by the 1862 International Exhibition, Liberty had opened his first shop at 218a Regent Street selling oriental furniture and china. Soon importing Japanese decorative work and fans, the business expanded rapidly, taking over many small adjacent premises. By the 1920s, however, the whole was in need of total redevelopment which was when his nephew, Captain Stewart Liberty, called in the Halls.

Their bipartite design, incorporating both Classical and Tudor forms, apparently arose out of a requirement to accommodate the conflicting demands of a canny retailer needing large windows and the more conservative opinions of the planning controllers retained by the Crown Commissioners. Thus on the Regent Street side Liberty was given the big display windows he required, along with a smart Portland stone façade incorporating giant Ionic pillars and an elaborate frieze. On the Great Marlborough Street side, meanwhile, the Halls created a vast black and white edifice linked by an arched bridge over Kingly Street to the Regent Street store. This was constructed inside and out using timbers from two of the Navy's last wooden ships, HMS *Hindustan* and HMS *Impregnable*, the one launched in 1824 just as Nash was completing his Regent Street scheme and the other in 1865 when it was reputed to be the largest wooden vessel afloat.

The critics are right, though, for it doesn't really work. The scale is wrong and at best it looks like a much later exercise in kitsch. (This is in part due to fussy detailing like the clock on the bridge and the little figures of St George and the dragon.) However, the craftsmanship throughout is honest, the materials where possible were hand-worked, the wood all correctly mortised and held together by pegs, and the Portland stone chiselled, not carved, by Italian artisans. The stained glass, similarly, was created by Liberty's own craftsmen.

It is significant too that after 130 years the store has retained its identity and much of its integrity. In the early days the likes of Whistler, Burne-Jones, Alma-Tadema and Rossetti were among Arthur Liberty's customers, and today people still visit a store expecting to find goods as individual and often as expertly made as the buildings from which they are sold.

POST OFFICE TOWER

HOWLAND STREET, W1

Afeter more than forty years, during which time it has changed names as many times as the telecommunications group for which it was commissioned in the first place, it is easy to take this one for granted. Nevertheless, it was a sad day for London when, in 1981, the Ministry of Works' truly iconic design for Britain's tallest building was finally eclipsed by the only slightly taller NatWest Tower. That one is cantilevered and technically extremely clever but to the average onlooker it appeared to be just another office block in the City. By contrast, the Post Office Tower, forged in the very core of Harold Wilson's 'white hot technological revolution', was from the start something special and rather distinctive.

Conceived by architect Eric Bedford and his team to soar above the noise and pollution of central London, the tower had a very specific function, namely as a support structure for dozens of dishes and aerials designed to beam high frequency or microwave radio, telephone and television signals above the raised edges of the London basin and across the country. Indeed, even now virtually every picture on British television screens passes through the tower which is still the world's largest video-switching platform.

To achieve all this Bedford designed a 580ft tower topped by a slender 39ft mast, essentially just a hollow concrete column rising from a more conventional, eight-storey base of offices. Designed to sway nearly eight inches from the vertical in high winds, his building also shrinks in height by a full nine inches in particularly cold weather. In order to disguise the concrete the length of the column was clad in steel and glass thereby giving it the appearance of a slender, circular office block. This was something not considered necessary for the many similar telecommunications towers erected in other major cities around the country at that time, such as the one in Birmingham, for example, which with its great flat surfaces of raw concrete still looks pretty brutal even today. Bedford's solution, however, works well although it was dismissed as clumsy by some critics and dishonest by those who espoused a purer, more function-driven approach to building design.

A successful illusion, it also conceals the fact that the quantity of accommodation provided within the building was never more than very modest. Indeed, very little was offered in the upper reaches of the tower other than an expensive revolving restaurant – a huge novelty for its day, the 30-ton section spinning through 360 degrees every twenty-two minutes at a speed of 0.11mph – and a couple of levels of observation decks. One of these was open to the elements and proved particularly popular with tourists seeking a genuine bird's-eye view of the capital, but sadly, like the revolving restaurant, both were closed to the public after the tower was damaged by IRA bombers in 1971. Today, a sad loss of amenity, all three levels are accessible only to guests and employees of BT.

PRINCE HENRY'S ROOM

FLEET STREET, EC4

A rare survivor of the Great Fire of 1666, London's only complete remaining timber-framed Jacobean town house was built half a century before the conflagration. Subsequently it suffered at the hands of a succession of insensitive occupiers before being rescued and restored by London County Council in 1898.

The site had a fascinating history preceding the seventeenth century. Originally a part of the great twelfth-century estate of the Knights Templar – the stone gateway beneath is still the entrance to Inner Temple – a few years after 1312, when the Templars' Order was dissolved, it was taken over by another Order, that of St John of Jerusalem (or the Knights Hospitallers). They leased the majority of the accommodation to lawyers, many of whom were already active in this area, while the rooms fronting on to Fleet Street were let to sundry other tenants.

By the early sixteenth century, however, at least half the site had found a new use as the Hand Inn, at which time the rooms above the gateway were already trading as the Prince's Arms with the innkeeper one Zachary Bennett. Following his death, his son John sold out to another publican, William Blake, who ordered the rebuilding in 1610–11. He renamed the whole the Prince's Arms in honour of James I's short-lived son, Henry (1594–1612), who became Prince of Wales that same year.

At the time of the Great Fire the inn had been renamed The Fountain and later the premises were taken over by Mrs Salmon's Waxworks. This was a hugely successful enterprise in a street which, by the close of the eighteenth century, was as well known for entertainments and exhibitions of the bizarre as it was for its enduring association with the printing and publishing trades. Established prior to 1711, and still trading into the reign of Queen Victoria (the owner herself died in 1760, aged ninety), popular exhibits at Mrs Salmon's included clockwork waxworks, one with a foot operated by lever which would kick passers-by and another of 'Margaret Countess of Heningbergh, Lying on a Bed of State, with her Three Hundred and Sixty-Five children, all born at one Birth'.

By 1898, perhaps unsurprisingly, the building itself was in a poor state, very dilapidated, its frontage boarded up and the ancient timbers covered in successive layers of paint. At a cost of some £30,000 it was carefully restored by the London County Council; the task was completed in 1906. All the exterior woodwork was also renewed except for the eight blackened oak panels on the upper floor which formed part of the original decoration.

Fortunately, though, the main room above the gateway has survived intact and unaltered, complete with some elegant panelling and an elaborate Jacobean plasterwork ceiling incorporating the initials P.H. and the would-be heir to the throne's three feathers. Popularly supposed to have at one time been the council chamber of the Duchy of Cornwall, although there is no evidence to support this view, the room is open to the public most afternoons.

STAPLE INN

1–3 HIGH HOLBORN, WC1

Today just four Inns of Court survive – Lincoln's, Gray's, and Middle and Inner Temple – but, originally called the Inns of Chancery, they were at one time far more numerous. Their original function has never been entirely understood, nor indeed is the derivation of the name clear, although it is thought that they may in earlier times have been involved in the training of medieval Chancery clerks who were charged with preparing the writs in the King's court.

In about 1530, however, a process of consolidation started as the previously named quartet began to exercise a greater degree of control over the many smaller Honourable Societies. Including Barnard's, Clement's, Clifford's, Furnival's, Lyon's, New and Staple, these smaller entities had by this time become little more than preparatory schools for those wishing to read for the law. Denied the right to call their own students to the Bar, each had over many years witnessed a gradual leaking away of student numbers as would-be lawyers enrolled instead with the main four.

Whatever its original purpose, it is known that Staple Inn was founded in 1378. It took its name from the building's previous function as a weighing-place and warehouse for wool, and as an important meeting place for merchants involved with the valuable wool trade. As a legal entity, though, it was eventually absorbed into Gray's Inn (which had acquired the freehold of the site in 1529), leaving a range of buildings still more or less intact behind this spectacular sixteenth-century façade of shops and offices. As such it remains by far the most impressive example of a half-timbered structure in London, this despite being much altered and restored over the years by a succession of new owners.

A portion of it, for example, was sold off by Gray's Inn in 1884 and went to house the Patent Office, while the Prudential spent £68,000 acquiring the majority which it restored over the next two to three years. At this time it was let to the Institute of Actuaries, but in 1944 much of the Prudential's work was undone by a German V1 which fell into the adjacent gardens. This necessitated an almost total rebuild, completed by Sir Edward Maufe in 1952, prompting some architectural historians to dismiss it as merely pastiche, a picturesque if somewhat unreliable example of Tudor urban building.

Nevertheless, the overall effect today is still striking and, with its oriel windows and jettied upper storeys overhanging a busy modern thoroughfare, it certainly manages to convey an image of a centuries-old London streetscape. An attractive evocation of what entire streets must have looked like nearly 500 years ago, nothing in London can quite match it.

THE GHERKIN

30 ST MARY AXE, EC3

Officially the Swiss Re Building, but known everywhere as The Gherkin, Foster & Partners' highly original 2004 RIBA Stirling Prize winner has very rapidly joined Big Ben, the Routemaster bus and Tower Bridge as one of London's universally recognised landmarks. Inevitably the 590ft building has its detractors, not least among them the many who resented the removal of the Grade II* Baltic Exchange which occupied the site before being bombed by the IRA. Generally, though, its surprising contours have made it one of central London's more popular modern buildings, even though initially at least some of the forty or so floors took some time to let.

Certainly it makes for a more interesting vista than many more conventional city blocks, not a few of them also from the drawing board of Norman Foster. And even if its claims to be environmentally progressive do not for some go quite far enough – it makes no attempt, for example, to harness either wind or solar energy – it offers its occupants natural ventilation using windows which open and close automatically, and plenty of sunlight in the manner of most tall, thin buildings.

At the same time it reportedly consumes up to 50 per cent less energy than many buildings the same size. Its distinctive cigar-like shape maximises the available daylight on the upper floors while the 258,000sq. ft exterior shell, comprising three layers of glass (the outer layer being double-glazed), encloses a ventilated cavity with computer-controlled blinds. To operate these a series of weather sensors constantly monitor external conditions such as temperature, sunlight levels and even wind speed before directing the blinds to close and windows to open as necessary.

Unfortunately, especially given its huge popularity, this genuinely radical building is not open to the public, and its restaurant, presently London's highest, is only for the use of tenants and their guests. The public can at least enjoy the curves, however, which being softer than its neighbours reduce the impact on its surroundings. In addition the building's tapering shape is also said to reduce the high winds frequently experienced at pavement level in heavily built-up areas.

As for the old Baltic Exchange, at the time of writing it was still in bits, boxed up in a barn near Canterbury. Having cost £4 million to dismantle, record and move, Britain's biggest box of Lego is for sale at £750,000 from a company called Pavilions of Splendour in Winchester. 'Ready to make a fine country house,' says the blurb, the carefully organised rubble comprising many tons of now de-listed red granite, coloured marble and Portland stone, complete with sea monsters and mermaids riding dolphins to grace the interior.

EPILOGUE: IF ONLY

Six Favourites That Never Made It

The National Gallery extension in Trafalgar Square was once famously likened to a carbuncle on the face of an old friend. Lord Palumbo's new Mansion House development has been described as looking like a pastel-coloured submarine. And more than fifteen years after the design was first unveiled, the Lloyds Building's external intestines continue to arouse as much irritation as they do delight.

Yet generally the capital's most controversial buildings – and in many cases its most fantastic designs – have been the ones which were never built. Work on a few of them was started but never finished. Others reached the final planning stages before events overtook them. William Kent's stupendous new Houses of Parliament, for example, was all cupolas and classical columns until it was sidelined by the famous 'War of Jenkins' Ear' (1739–42) with Spain. Most must have seemed doomed from the start: like the Primrose Hill Pyramid which would have dwarfed the Egyptian originals with space for more than five million dead, or, as we saw earlier, the scheme hatched after the death of Prince Albert to up-end his mighty Crystal Palace to form a unique 1,000ft tall memorial to him in Hyde Park.

Even many of those architectural landmarks one now takes for granted were initially conceived to be otherwise and only gradually evolved into the familiar form we see today. It was originally proposed, for example, that Lord Nelson stand not at the top but at the foot of his column, as once he had stood before the mast. One of Wren's initial sketches for St Paul's showed a huge pineapple atop the stately dome – the exotic fruit was all the rage, having just started arriving from the West Indies – and as late as 1918 American shopping magnate Gordon Selfridge hoped to mount a square tower on top of his building in Oxford Street. In fact the one he proposed was so massive it would almost certainly have caused his famous store to collapse.

Then as now, extraordinary buildings seem inevitably to require extraordinary men. The aptly named Batty Langley, for example, designed a new Mansion House for the City with no windows and such an overabundance of Masonic motifs that it was dismissed out of hand, while an Irish MP, Colonel (later Sir) Frederick Trench, persisted for decades with his own schemes despite being publicly ridiculed for his ideas. These included building another **giant pyramid** – this one to cover the whole of Trafalgar Square – and an immense new royal palace, approached along an avenue several hundred feet wide, stretching from Hyde Park to the City. It would have required the demolition along the way of Covent Garden, the Crusaders' ancient Temple Church and much of the West End.

Nor was Trench even slightly discouraged by Queen Victoria's insistence that she was quite happy with her existing palace; like so many of London's would-be remodellers he was happy enough with his own fantasies. Equally it could surely have been only fantasy for the Greater London Council in 1967 to commission a feasibility study for the **Regent Street Monorail**, its plan being to erect twin overhead rails to carry passengers the length of one of London's more distinguished streets. Likewise, for Charles Glover to propose in 1931 the construction of the **King's Cross Aerodrome**. Nothing less than a giant six-spoked wheel a full half-mile in diameter, this was intended to sit balanced above the existing railway station, although even Mr Glover admitted that aircraft design would have to progress somewhat if anything was to land safely on one of his elevated spokes.

To such visionaries as these, nothing seemed sacred and nothing was to remain unchanged. In the 1880s John Leighton seriously suggested redrawing the boundaries of every London borough so that each one would be hexagonal, and a century earlier a House of Commons Committee spent several days considering a barely credible plan to straighten the River Thames. The sponsor of this latter scheme, one Willey Reveley, proposed to dig a new channel nearly a mile long in order to save ships the time they had hitherto been forced to waste sailing round the Isle of Dogs.

Since then it has often been argued, indeed is still being argued, that the capital does not make the most of this river – but if so it is certainly not for want of ideas. Architect W.F.C. Holden, for example, argued that by rebuilding **Tower Bridge in glass** he would improve the view as well as reducing the need for constant repainting, while numerous other elaborate or ingenious schemes have sought to exploit the Thames in different ways.

That most respected engineer Robert Stephenson, for example, approved plans for the Thames Viaduct Railway, a giant latticework of steel enabling trains to run down the centre of the river. Several eminent Victorians favoured schemes to dam the Thames at Woolwich to create a giant inner-city freshwater lake. In 1861 an architect called Harry Newton suggested building a pair of massive mid-stream islands to accommodate new government offices, the central law courts and some private luxury apartments. He withdrew his plans only when asked how much all this would cost.

Perhaps the most extraordinary scheme, if only because construction work actually began, was **Wembley's own Eiffel Tower**. As early as 1869 an entrepreneur called Sir Edward Watkin had proposed digging a tunnel under the English Channel, indeed had commenced digging the thing under the Kent coast, before it was pointed out he had not obtained the necessary permissions to do so. Instead, no lover of France, and in the belief that anything Paris could do we could do bigger and better, he set out to out-Eiffel the Eiffel Tower.

Establishing the Metropolitan Tower Construction Company, and soliciting financial support from many thousands of loyal subscribers, Sir Edward proposed to present London with a tower at least 150ft taller than Gustave Eiffel's 984-footer. (Cheekily he even suggested M. Eiffel tender a design of his own, but the Frenchman declined on patriotic grounds.) Dozens of ideas were tendered, flooding in from as far afield as Sweden, Turkey and Australia. They included one similar to the Leaning Tower of Pisa, only standing upright, and another bedecked with hanging gardens and intended to house a community of high-altitude vegetarians.

The winner, to whom Sir Edward awarded a handsome prize of 500 guineas, suggested erecting a virtual copy of Gustave Eiffel's edifice and in 1891 work began on 280 acres of grassy Wembley that Sir Edward had acquired for this purpose.

More than 100,000 people came to see the work in progress but it quickly became apparent that public patriotism and Sir Edward's optimism were not sufficient drivers to get the job done. Money was short – with the tower standing at barely 150ft, the remaining balance of subscriptions was clearly inadequate for another thousand – and the tower quickly became known as 'the Shareholders' Dismay'. Before long there were calls for Sir Edward to recompense Londoners for spoiling their views with his ugly stump, and while this did not happen work soon stopped altogether.

For a dozen years or more his folly quietly rusted away, its scrap value estimated to be unequal to the cost of demolition. Perhaps the sums balanced after a while, however, for in 1907 fewer than a dozen people turned up to see a firm of Mancunian demolition experts put bolts of dynamite beneath the tower's four steel legs and blow the whole ensemble to bits. Fortunately Watkin was long dead and today Wembley's new stadium stands in its place.

But at least England's tower had been intended for an empty site. In 1861 the Liberal parliamentarian Acton Ayrton had solemnly proposed pulling down Henry VIII's 'goodly manor', the then 350-year-old St James's Palace, and building in its place a new university.

That same year an Irish impresario by the name of Dion Boucicault threated to spoil forever the view from Westminster by erecting on the south bank the Victorian equivalent of a theme park – complete with rooftop dining, rocky grottoes and waterfalls, even a miniature Alpine scene complete with tree-clad, snow-capped mountains. John Davis-Paine designed a new Royal Exchange so huge that its construction would have necessitated the complete destruction of the Bank of England.

John Goldicutt, meanwhile, had designs on the very heart of the empire. Having failed to oust Nelson's likeness from Trafalgar Square in favour of his own immense statue of William IV, in 1841 he proposed filling the square with a replica **Roman Colosseum**. Rising to four or five storeys, Goldicutt claimed his vast elliptical warren could provide a permanent home for the Royal Academy as well as for various learned societies of literature, science, astronomy and geology. Happily, and as he had at Trafalgar, Nelson prevailed and stands there still. As recently as 1959 another favourite spot came close to annihilation when a Birmingham developer secured planning permission to plonk a faceless, almost windowless, twenty-storey block on top of Piccadilly Circus. Then came New Labour's Millennium Dome, which, although actually built, is probably no more or less extraordinary than some of Colonel Trench's follies – and certainly no less expensive. At the time of writing the Millennium Dome remains empty and unloved by Londoners, who, like most city dwellers, tend generally to be careless of their surroundings but still know a good building when they see it and rarely, if ever, warm to the other sort.

BIBLIOGRAPHY

Unless otherwise stated all books are published in London.

Ackroyd, P., *London: The Biography*, Chatto & Windus, 2000
Ash, R., *The Londoner's Almanac*, Century, 1985
Aslet, C., *The Story of Greenwich*, Fourth Estate, 1999
Atkinson, H.D., *English Architecture*, Methuen, 1926
Barker, F. and Hyde, R., *London as It Might Have Been*, John Murray, 1995
Barker, F. and Silvester-Carr, D., *The Black Plaque Guide to London*, Constable, 1987
Barrow, A., *Gossip*, New York, Coward, McCann & Geoghegan, 1978
Beard, G., *The Work of John Vanbrugh*, New York, Universe Books, 1986
Booker, C. and Lycett Green, C., *Goodbye London*, Fontana, 1973
Bruce, A., *Keepers of the Kingdom*, New York, Vendome Press, 1999
Cahill, K., *Who Owns Britain*, Edinburgh, Canongate, 2001
Churchill, W., *The Second World War*, Cassell, 1948
Clunn, H.P., *The Face of London*, Spring Books, 1957
Colson, P., *White's 1693–1950*, Heinemann, 1951
Colvin, H., *Royal Buildings*, RIBA/Country Life, 1968
Cornforth, J., *The Search for a Style*, WW Norton, 1988
Crewe, Q., *Crewe House*, Stacey International, 1995
Culbertson, J. and Randall, T., *Permanent Londoners*, Robson, 2000
Cunningham, P., *Change of Use*, A & C Black, 1988
Deighton, L., *Len Deighton's London Dossier*, Jonathan Cape, 1967
Dictionary of National Biography, Oxford, Oxford University Press, 1975
Dixon, R. and Muthesius, S., *Victorian Buildings*, Thames & Hudson, 1978
Douet, J., *British Barracks*, English Heritage/HMSO, 1998
Duncan, A., *Secret London*, New Holland, 2003
—— *Walking Haunted London*, New Holland, 1999
Ellmers, C. and Werner, A., *London's Lost Riverscape*, Viking, 1988
Fairfield, S., *The Streets of London*, Papermac, 1983
Fellows, R., *Edwardian Architecture*, Aldershot, Lund Humphries, 1995
Fletcher, G., *London at My Feet*, Daily Telegraph, 1980
Foreman, S., *From Palace to Power*, Brighton, Alpha Press, 1995
Forrest, D., *St James's Square*, Quiller Press, 2001
Friedman, J., *Inside London*, Phaidon, 1988
Girouard, M., *Cities and People*, New Haven, Yale University Press, 1985
Glancey, J., *Twentieth-century Architecture*, Carlton, 1998
Graves, C., *Leather Armchairs*, Cassell, 1963
Halliday, S., *Making the Metropolis*, Derby, Breedon, 2003

Headley, G. and Meulencamp, W., *Follies*, Aurum, 1999
Hibbert, C., *London: Biography of a City*, Longmans, 1969
—— and Weinreb, B., *The London Encyclopaedia*, Macmillan, 1983
HRH The Prince of Wales, *A Vision of Britain*, Doubleday, 1989
Inwood, S., *A History of London*, Macmillan, 1998
Jenkins, S., *City at Risk*, Hutchinson, 1970
—— *England's Thousand Best Houses*, Allen Lane, 2003
Jenner, M., *London Heritage*, Michael Joseph, 1988
Johnson, N., *Eighteenth-century London*, Norwich, HMSO, 1991
Jones, B., *Follies and Grottoes*, Constable, 1974
Jones, E. and Woodward, C., *A Guide to the Architecture of London*, Seven Dials, 2000
Kent, W., *An Encyclopaedia of London*, Dent, 1970
Lambton, L., *Curious Houses*, Chatto & Windus, 1988
le Vay, B., *Eccentric London*, Chalfont St Peter, Bradt, 2002
Lees-Milne, J., *Midway on the Waves*, Michael Russell, 2005
Lejeune, A., *The Gentlemen's Clubs of London*, Parkgate, 1997
Macmillan, I. and Baker, R., *The Book of London*, Michael Joseph, 1969
Mee, A., *London*, Hodder & Stoughton, 1937
Montgomery-Massingberd, H. (ed.), *Lord of the Dance*, Debrett's, 1986
Mordaunt Crook, J., *The Greek Revival*, RIBA/Country Life, 1968
—— *The Rise of the Nouveaux Riches*, John Murray, 1999
Morton, H.V., *H.V. Morton's London*, Methuen, 1940
—— *In Search of London*, Methuen, 1951
Paxman, J., *Friends in High Places*, Michael Joseph, 1990
Pearce, D., *The Great Houses of London*, New York, Vendome Press, 1986
Pevsner, N., *Buildings of England: London*, 2 vols, Penguin, 1952, 1962
Rennison, N., *The Blue Plaque Guide*, 2nd edn, Stroud, Sutton, 2003
Renwick, E.D., *Order of St John*, St John's Gate, 1958
Roebuck, J., *Urban Development in Nineteenth-century London*, Chichester, Phillimore, 1979
Rose, N., *The Cliveden Set*, Jonathan Cape, 2000
Russell, J., *London*, New York, Harry N. Abrams, 1994
Saint, A. (ed.), *London Suburbs*, English Heritage/Merrell Holberton, 1999
Sampson, A., *Anatomy of Britain*, Hodder & Stoughton, 1962
Saunders, A., *St Paul's*, Collins & Brown, 2001
—— *The Art and Architecture of London*, Phaidon, 1988
Sinclair, I., *Lights out for the Territory*, Granta, 1997
Smith, S., *Underground London*, Abacus, 2004
Snowdon, Lord, *London Sight Unseen*, Weidenfeld & Nicolson, 1999
Soane, J., *New Home*, Conran Octopus, 2003
Summerson, J., *Georgian London*, New Haven, Yale University Press, 2003
Sykes, C.S., *Private Palaces*, Chatto & Windus, 1985
Thorold, H., *Ruined Abbeys of England*, Scotland and Wales, HarperCollins, 1993
Thorrold, P., *The London Rich*, Viking, 1999
Trench, R. and Hillman, E., *London Under London*, John Murray, 1984
Watson-Smythe, M. (ed.), *Deserted Bastions*, SAVE Britain's Heritage, 1993
Williams, G., *Stronghold Britain*, Stroud, Sutton, 1999

INDEX